First World War
and Army of Occupation
War Diary
France, Belgium and Germany

14 DIVISION
Divisional Troops
61 Field Company Royal Engineers
20 May 1915 - 31 May 1919

WO95/1889/1

The Naval & Military Press Ltd
www.nmarchive.com
Published in association with The National Archives

Published by

The Naval & Military Press Ltd

Unit 10 Ridgewood Industrial Park,

Uckfield, East Sussex,

TN22 5QE England

Tel: +44 (0) 1825 749494

www.naval-military-press.com

www.nmarchive.com

Contents

Document type	Place/Title	Date From	Date To
Heading	WO95/1889/1		
Heading	14th Division 61st Field Coy. R.E. May 1915-May 1919		
Heading	War Diary Of 61st Field Company Royal Engineers From 20.5.1915 To 31.5.1915 to 20-31.5.15 vol I 20-31.5.15 14 Division		
War Diary	Aldershot	20/05/1915	20/05/1915
War Diary	Southampton	20/05/1915	20/05/1915
War Diary	Haure	21/05/1915	23/05/1915
War Diary	Wulverdinghe	24/05/1915	31/05/1915
Heading	14th Division 61st 7.C.R.E. Vol II 1-30.6.15		
War Diary	Vlamertinghe	01/06/1915	04/06/1915
War Diary	Dickebusch	05/06/1915	19/06/1915
War Diary	Squal L 20 Sheet 27	20/06/1915	30/06/1915
Heading	14th Division 61st F.C.R.E. Vol III July 15		
War Diary	H.7.A.1.4	01/07/1915	02/07/1915
Heading	14th Division 61st F.C.R.E. Vol IV August 15		
War Diary	H F A	01/08/1915	31/08/1915
Heading	14th Division 61st F.C.R.E. Vol. V Sept. 15		
War Diary	H F A	01/09/1915	07/09/1915
War Diary	Ara 33	08/09/1915	30/09/1915
Heading	14th Division 61st F.C.R.E. Vol. 6 Oct 15		
War Diary	Ara 33	01/10/1915	31/10/1915
Heading	14th Division 61st F.C.R.E. Vol 7 Nov 15		
War Diary	H F A	01/11/1915	30/11/1915
Heading	14th Div 61st F.C.R.E. Vol 8 Dec 1915		
War Diary	Ara 3.3	01/12/1915	31/12/1915
Heading	14th Div 61st F.C.R.E Vol 9 Jan 1916		
War Diary		01/01/1916	31/01/1916
Heading	14th 61st F.C.R.E. Vol 10		
War Diary	Brandhoek	01/02/1916	12/02/1916
War Diary	Dudezeele	13/02/1916	22/02/1916
War Diary	Flesselles	23/02/1916	25/02/1916
War Diary	Sus St Leger	26/02/1916	27/02/1916
War Diary	Fosseux	28/02/1916	29/02/1916
Heading	14 61 F.C.R.E. Vol 11		
Miscellaneous	Officer 1/ C A E S office Base	04/04/1916	04/04/1916
War Diary	Fosseux	01/03/1916	01/03/1916
War Diary	Dainville	02/03/1916	03/03/1916
War Diary	Arras	04/03/1916	04/03/1916
War Diary	Dainville	05/03/1916	12/03/1916
War Diary	Arras	13/03/1916	13/03/1916
War Diary	Dainville	13/03/1916	13/03/1916
War Diary	Berneville	13/03/1916	13/03/1916
War Diary	Arras	14/03/1916	14/03/1916
War Diary	Berneville Simencourt	14/03/1916	31/03/1916
War Diary	Dainville	17/03/1916	29/03/1916
War Diary	Arras Blanc	01/04/1916	30/04/1916
War Diary	Cemetery		
War Diary	Ry Bank N Of Cemetert		

War Diary	St Saveur		
War Diary	Arras	01/04/1916	17/04/1916
War Diary	Arras	01/04/1916	30/04/1916
Miscellaneous	61st Field C.R.E. 14 Div War Diary April 1916 Appendix No I	02/04/1916	02/04/1916
Miscellaneous	Sectional Elevation Of O.P. Appendix I Sheet III		
Diagram etc	Appendix No II S.A.A. Store		
Miscellaneous	Appendix No III	02/05/1916	02/05/1916
Diagram etc	Vertical Section of Arch Lining Cave		
Diagram etc	Plan showing arrangement of reinforcement		
Miscellaneous	Appendix No IV Report On O.P. in S.T. sauveur	02/05/1916	02/05/1916
Diagram etc	Sectional Elevation Of O.P. (Side View)		
Miscellaneous	Sectional Elevation Of O.P. (Front View)		
War Diary	Arras	01/05/1916	04/05/1916
War Diary	Wanquentin	01/05/1916	22/05/1916
Map			
Heading	61st Field C.R.E. 14th Division War Diary April 1916 Appendix I Map of Section		
War Diary	Wanquentin	01/05/1916	31/05/1916
War Diary	Dainville	01/06/1916	01/06/1916
Miscellaneous	Offices i/c	03/07/1916	03/07/1916
War Diary	Wanquetin	01/06/1916	05/06/1916
War Diary	Wanquetin To Dainville	06/06/1916	06/06/1916
War Diary	To Arras To Agny To Dainville	07/06/1916	07/06/1916
War Diary	Arras Agny Dainville	08/06/1916	17/06/1916
War Diary	To Arras to Agny to Dainville	17/06/1916	17/06/1916
War Diary	Arras	19/06/1916	30/06/1916
War Diary		01/07/1917	31/07/1917
Heading	14th Division 61st Field Company Royal Engineers August 1916		
Miscellaneous	Herewith Report in Yesterdays Operations as affecting this Company.	19/08/1916	19/08/1916
War Diary	Bonnieres	01/08/1916	01/08/1916
War Diary	Grimont	02/08/1916	07/08/1916
War Diary	Camp	08/08/1916	12/08/1916
War Diary	Mametz	13/08/1916	30/08/1916
War Diary	Dernancourt	31/08/1916	31/08/1916
War Diary	Boisrault	01/09/1916	16/09/1916
War Diary	Dernancourt	17/09/1916	22/09/1916
War Diary	Grouches	23/09/1916	27/09/1916
War Diary	Le Permont	28/09/1916	30/09/1916
War Diary	War Diary Of The 61st Field Coy R.E. From 1st October 1216 To 31st October 1916		
War Diary	Le Fermont		
Heading	War Diary Of 61st To Coy R.E. From 1st November To 30th November 1916 Volume I		
War Diary	Le Fermont	01/11/1916	05/11/1916
War Diary	Crouy En Arras	06/11/1916	23/11/1916
War Diary	Arras	24/11/1916	30/11/1916
War Diary	Arras	01/12/1916	08/12/1916
War Diary	Lignereuil	08/12/1916	27/12/1916
War Diary	Le Fermont	31/12/1916	31/12/1916
War Diary		02/12/1916	05/12/1916
Map	Proposed Plan Of Regimental And Post G.35 D.25.85		
War Diary	Lefermont F Sector	11/01/1917	23/01/1917
War Diary			

War Diary	Arras	05/02/1917	30/04/1917
Miscellaneous	14th Division	01/11/1917	01/11/1917
Heading	War Diary Of The 61st F.C.R.E. Coy R.E. 1st May 1917-31st May 1917		
War Diary	Arras	01/05/1917	31/05/1917
Miscellaneous	14th Division "A"	04/07/1917	04/07/1917
War Diary	Arras	01/07/1917	30/07/1917
War Diary	Vierstrat	01/07/1917	31/07/1917
War Diary		14/07/1917	20/07/1917
War Diary	Vierstrat	01/08/1917	06/08/1917
War Diary	Laestre	06/08/1917	15/08/1917
War Diary	Wippenhoek	16/08/1917	25/08/1917
War Diary	Busseboom	26/08/1917	31/08/1917
War Diary	Berthen Area	01/09/1917	04/09/1917
War Diary	Neuve Eglise	05/09/1917	12/10/1917
War Diary	Dickebusche	13/10/1917	11/11/1917
War Diary	Vlamertinghe	11/11/1917	12/11/1917
War Diary	Potize	13/11/1917	24/11/1917
Miscellaneous	C E VIII Corps No. 425 14th Divn No G.S. 1189 C.R.E 14th Divn No. 1427		
Miscellaneous	14th Divsn Has Much Pleasure In Forwarding The Above Letter For Information	10/11/1917	10/11/1917
War Diary	Potize	01/12/1917	02/12/1917
War Diary	Ypres	03/12/1917	30/12/1917
War Diary		21/12/1917	23/12/1917
War Diary		01/01/1918	24/01/1918
War Diary	Beines	24/01/1918	24/01/1918
War Diary	Jussy	25/01/1918	26/01/1918
War Diary	Dugouts	27/01/1918	27/01/1918
War Diary	Ravine Des Saules	28/01/1918	31/01/1918
War Diary	New Year Honours	31/01/1918	31/01/1918
War Diary	Ravine Des Saules Subracted between Essigny-Le-Grand & Benay about 5 Miles from St. Quentin	01/02/1918	05/02/1918
War Diary	About 5 Miles from St Quentin	08/02/1918	28/02/1918
Heading	14th Divisional Engineers 61st Field Company R.E. March 1918		
War Diary	Ravine Des Saules 1 Km West Of Benay	01/03/1918	20/03/1918
War Diary	Ravine Des Saules	20/03/1918	22/03/1918
War Diary	1 K.M. South Of Cugny	22/03/1918	23/03/1918
War Diary	Beaulieu	23/03/1918	24/03/1918
War Diary	Beines	24/03/1918	24/03/1918
War Diary	Buchoire	24/03/1918	24/03/1918
War Diary	Quesmy	24/03/1918	24/03/1918
War Diary	Croiselles	24/03/1918	24/03/1918
War Diary	Beaurains	24/03/1918	24/03/1918
War Diary	Lavignette	25/03/1918	25/03/1918
War Diary	Dive Le Franc	25/03/1918	25/03/1918
War Diary	Euricourt	25/03/1918	25/03/1918
War Diary	Thiescourt	25/03/1918	26/03/1918
War Diary	Elincourt	27/03/1918	27/03/1918
War Diary	Rouvillers	27/03/1918	28/03/1918
War Diary	Beaurepaire	29/03/1918	29/03/1918
War Diary	Nogent	30/03/1918	30/03/1918
War Diary	Bizancourt	31/03/1918	31/03/1918
Heading	14th Div. War Diary 61st Field Company, R.E. April 1918		

War Diary	Vellenes	01/04/1918	01/04/1918
War Diary	Flechy	02/04/1918	02/04/1918
War Diary	Vers	03/04/1918	03/04/1918
War Diary	Aubigny	04/04/1918	05/04/1918
War Diary	Blangy Tronville	05/04/1918	07/04/1918
War Diary	Aoliens	08/04/1918	09/04/1918
War Diary	Yzrengremer	10/04/1918	11/04/1918
War Diary	Wicquinghem	12/04/1918	14/04/1918
War Diary	Mollinghem	15/04/1918	01/06/1918
Diagram etc	Profile Where There Are Fire Steps		
Miscellaneous	Instructions For The Preparation Of Emergency Defensive Lines	07/04/1918	07/04/1918
Diagram etc	Breastwork Task Diagram (with Hurdle Revetment)		
Diagram etc	Breastwork Task Diagram (with Sod Revetment)		
Diagram etc	Dimensions Of Breastworks		
War Diary	Molinghem	01/07/1918	09/07/1918
War Diary	Setques	10/07/1918	13/07/1918
War Diary	Westrove	28/07/1918	31/07/1918
War Diary	Eeck Hout Casteel	01/08/1918	16/08/1918
War Diary	Broglandt Aved	17/08/1918	17/08/1918
War Diary	Proven	18/08/1918	18/08/1918
War Diary	Benwell Camp	19/08/1918	28/08/1918
War Diary	H12a 3.5.	01/09/1918	18/09/1918
War Diary		05/08/1918	06/08/1918
War Diary	H 12 A 3.5 Ypres.		
War Diary	H 12 A 3.5	05/09/1918	19/09/1918
War Diary	Busseboom	20/09/1918	15/10/1918
War Diary	Comines	16/10/1918	31/10/1918
Diagram etc	Lock Gate Bridge Commines		
Diagram etc	Plan Of Lock Gate Bridge		
Diagram etc	Cross Section Of Morte Lys Bridge		
Diagram etc	Damaged Building		
Diagram etc	Bridge Over River Douve At 28/ T3 b3.1.		
Miscellaneous	Cross Sections Of Bridge Over River Douve At 28/ T3 B 3.1.		
War Diary	Evregnies	01/11/1918	09/11/1918
War Diary	Evregnies	10/11/1918	17/11/1918
War Diary	Tourcoing	18/11/1918	20/11/1918
War Diary	Espierres	21/11/1918	01/02/1919
Heading	War Diary Of 61st Field Coy. R.E. 1-31st March, 1919		
War Diary	Tourcoing	01/03/1919	31/03/1919
Heading	War Diary Of 61st Field Coy. R.E. From 1st April, 1919. To: 30th April, 1919		
War Diary	Tourcoing	09/04/1919	29/04/1919
Heading	War Diary Of 61st Field Company. R.E. From: 1st May, 1919. To: 31st May, 1919.		
War Diary	Estampuis	01/05/1919	31/05/1919

14TH DIVISION

61ST FIELD COY. R..E.

MAY 1915 - MAY 1919

121/5505

CONFIDENTIAL

WAR DIARY
OF
61st FIELD COMPANY ROYAL ENGINEERS

FROM 20.5.1915 to 31.5.1915.

VOL. I. 20 — 31.5.15

14th Division.

May 19

Instructions regarding War Diaries and Intelligence Summaries are contained in F. S. Regs., Part II. and the Staff Manual respectively. Title pages will be prepared in manuscript.

WAR DIARY

or

~~INTELLIGENCE SUMMARY~~

(Erase heading not required.)

Army Form C. 2118.

61st Field Co R.E.

Hour, Date, Place	Summary of Events and Information	Remarks and references to Appendices
1.45 am / 2.55 am 20.5.15 Aldershot	Company entrained for Southampton. Strength 6 officers, 223 Other Ranks, 81 Horses & mules, 11 4-wheeled vehicles, 9 2-wheeled	
11 am to 1 pm 20.5.15 Southampton	Embarked at Southampton on MINNESOTA, less 1 officer & 68 men embarked on EMPRESS QUEEN	
4 am 21.5.15 Havre	Reached Havre Docks. disembarked 8 am Reached Camp 11 am	
11 am 23.5.15 Havre	Entrained at Gare des Marchandises Havre, the detachment of 1 officer & 68 men having rejoined Company at 12 noon on 22nd.	
4 pm. 24.5.15 WULVERDINGHE.	Detrained at ST OMER & marched 8 miles to billets at WULVERDINGHE.	
26.5.15	Marched at 9.30 am to billets near CONPERDU	with 41st Inf Bde.
27.5.15	Marched at 6.30 am to billets 1 mile N.E. of CAESTRE	with 41st Inf Bde
28.5.15	Marched at 6.30 am, joined 62nd Co R.E. at BEAUVOORDE at 9 am, & then under CRE 14 Div marched to VLAMERTINGHE which Coy reached at 1 pm. Detached from 14 Div for work under CRE V Corps.	
29.5.15	Coy working on defences of YPRES from LILLE Gate to MENIN Gate.	with 52nd & 63rd Cos Belgian workmen
30.5.15	Coy working on defences of YPRES round MENIN Gate northwards.	ditto
31.5.15	Coy working on defences of YPRES round MENIN GATE northwards.	ditto

S.P. Mahony Major R.E.
[illegible]

1247 W 3299 200,000 (E) 8/14 J.B.C. & A. Forms/C. 2118/11.

14th Division

181/58½

61st F. C. R. E.

Vol: II 1 — 30. 6. 15.

Instructions regarding War Diaries and Intelligence Summaries are contained in F. S. Regs., Part II. and the Staff Manual respectively. Title pages will be prepared in manuscript.

WAR DIARY

~~or~~

~~INTELLIGENCE SUMMARY~~

(Erase heading not required.)

Army Form C. 2118.

61st Field Co RE.

Hour, Date, Place	Summary of Events and Information	Remarks and references to Appendices
June 1915		
1st to 3rd. VLAMERTINGHE	Worked on defences of YPRES round MENIN GATE northwards to Canal. with the 52nd & 63rd Coys Belgian Travailleurs under us on northern Trenches.	
4th VLAMERTINGHE	awaiting orders to move.	
5 DICKEBUSCH	marched 6.30 am to LA CLYTTE & then back to Canada Huts near DICKEBUSCH which reached 1pm. Quarters in Huts except No 2 section in dugouts & Horses wagons bivouaced. Section officers visited Trenches.	
6 DICKEBUSCH	Sections worked on front line trenches held by 83rd Infy Bde. No 3 by day rest by night.	41st Inf Bde took over trenches from 83rd Inf Bde on night 7-8
7 "	ditto.	Brigadier General Nugent i/c of Section M2 to P4b.
8 "	all sections worked by night on front line Trenches now held by 41st Inf Bde. No 1 section on right, No 3 on left. No 2 supporting line on right, Gave 1 NCO & sappers to Lt Taylor for work at BOIS CONFLUENT. mining purposes.	
9 "	ditto	
10 "	{ ditto Commenced support trench between M1 & M2. Continued work improving Communication Trench through BOIS CONFLUENT & improving P4 fire trench.	
~~11~~ "	~~ditto~~	
11th	Work at night 7pm to 5am. Wet day. Trenches very muddy. Commenced Commn Trench between M4 & N7, and between N11 and S7 & Improved fire trenches P1 and P2 & through BOIS CONFLUENT & had infantry & Cavalry working Party along Switch at DIEPENDAAL BEEK with No 4 section.	Cbm Capt RE. The officers of infantry working Party between M4 & N7 and of Cyclist working Party at Switch were wounded also one infantry Sergeant.

1247 W 3299 200,000 (E) 8/14 J.B.C. & A. Forms/C. 2118/11.

Instructions regarding War Diaries and Intelligence Summaries are contained in F. S. Regs., Part II. and the Staff Manual respectively. Title pages will be prepared in manuscript.

WAR DIARY

or

~~INTELLIGENCE SUMMARY~~

(Erase heading not required.)

Army Form C. 2118

61st Field Co. R.E

(2)

Hour, Date, Place	Summary of Events and Information	Remarks and references to Appendices
12th DICKEBUSCH	Repair Communication trench BRASSERIE to BOIS CONFLUENT and working on support & communication trenches. Switch in BOIS CONFLUENT	81st Inf Bde relieved 44th Inf Bde in trenches night 12-13th
13th Dickebusch	Constructing Communication Trenches M4 to N7 and N11 to S7 and support trench in rear M1 & M2. Improving fire trench P4 and converting Comm. Trenches near P3 into fire trenches & improving various Comm. Trenches. Spr Hall wounded. Erecting 2 Canvas Screens west of WYTCHETEBEEK.	Brigadier Genl. Bols Comdg 84th Inf Bde – charge of Sector M2 to P4b.
14th DICKEBUSCH	Constructing Comm. Trench through BOIS CARRE, improving P4 Trench, and Comm. Trench through BOIS CONFLUENT. Constructing fire trench for Switch near O5 and BOIS CONFLUENT. Lt Taylor RE failed to fire the Camouflets at P3. Extending Comm. Trench from BRASSERIE Entrance to Main	Comm. Trenches } under orders of CRE 28th Div from 6pm on 14th
15th DICKEBUSCH	Constructing Comm. Trenches through BOIS CARRE & improving that through BOIS CONFLUENT, Erecting screen on road near BRASSERIE, helping Lt Taylor at Camouflets near P3 of which he fired one at 3.45 am. Continuing building up support trench in rear of M1 M2. Heavy firing during night on sector to our right.	
16th DICKEBUSCH	Working on support trench behind M1 M2, constructing Comm. Trench thro BOIS CARRE connecting Comm. Trench at P2 with fire trench, drainage of BOIS CONFLUENT and work on Switch fire trenches near O5.	[illegible] Capt RE

1247 W 3299 200,000 (E) 8/14 J.B.C. & A. Forms/C. 2118/11.

(3)

WAR DIARY

or

~~INTELLIGENCE SUMMARY~~

(Erase heading not required.)

Instructions regarding War Diaries and Intelligence Summaries are contained in F. S. Regs., Part II. and the Staff Manual respectively. Title pages will be prepared in manuscript.

Army Form C. 2118.

61st Field Co RE

Hour, Date, Place	Summary of Events and Information	Remarks and references to Appendices
17/6/15 DICKEBUSCH	Improving Fire and Commnt Trenches about O2. Constructing Commnt Trench through BOIS CARRE. Constructing Fire Trenches for Switch near O5 and S8.	200 infantry as working party. 1 man wounded.
18/6/15 DICKEBUSCH	Improving Commnt Trench between O2 & O3, and through Bois CONFLUENT and BOIS CARRE. Constructing Fire Trenches at Switch through Bois and near O5. Handed over RE work in Sector to OC 38th Fd Coy RE.	No infantry working parties available thro relief of trenches.
19/6/15 DICKEBUSCH	~~Marched at 9.30 am to billets near ABEELE about 8 miles which was reached about 1.30 pm.~~ No 4 section worked at traverses in Commnt Trench through Bois CONFLUENT, not relieved.	Spr. Hodgkiss wounded by shrapnel in Commn Trench.
7pm		
20/6/15 Sheet L 20 Sheet 27	Marched from DICKEBUSCH 9.30 am and billeted in farms near ABEELE at 1.30 pm. fine.	
21/6/15 — do —	Rested in Billets.	
22/6/15 — do —	Marched to field 1½ miles west of VLAMERTINGE where started building dugouts.	
23/6/15 — do —	Continued building shelters & dugouts for Company obtaining materials from YPRES and RE Park. Capt Chesney, Lt Jarrett Smith reconnoitred the trenches. No 1 section working RE 1st Bst Park	
24/6/15 — do —	No 3 section with 8th RB (600) men as working party paraded 6.30 pm and assembled at ECOLE East of YPRES for work on Commnt and assembly Trenches. Major Mackenzie appointed to act as CRE East of YPRES. Nos 1, 2 Sections worked on Dugouts. No 3 at RE Park.	
25/6/15 — do —	Raining heavily. Working party did not go to trenches, men continued dugouts.	C... Capt RE

1247 W 3299 200,000 (E) 8/14 J.B.C. & A. Forms/C. 2118/11.

WAR DIARY
or
INTELLIGENCE SUMMARY
(Erase heading not required.)

Army Form C. 2118.

Instructions regarding War Diaries and Intelligence Summaries are contained in F. S. Regs., Part II. and the Staff Manual respectively. Title pages will be prepared in manuscript.

Hour, Date, Place		Summary of Events and Information	Remarks and references to Appendices
26/6/15.	—do—	No 1 & 2 Sections paraded 6.30 p.m. Met infantry working party 800 men at École & worked on communication & assembly trenches.	
27/6/15	—do—	No 3 & 4 Sections paraded 6.30 p.m. Met infantry working party of 800 men at École & worked on communication & assembly trenches.	
28/6/15.	—do—	No 1 & 2 Sections paraded 6.45 p.m. Met infantry working party of 800 men at École. ½ Coy of Infantry carried up trench boards (50) & pickets for trenches. ~~Remainder with sappers worked on Communication & Assembly trenches.~~ Bombardment commenced at 11 p.m. & working parties returned as area was unsafe. Sappers worked on dugouts till actual bombardment commenced, stayed it out & returned on completion at 12.30 a.m.	
29/6/15	—do—	Nos 3 & 4 Sections paraded 6.45 p.m. & worked on Communication trench. No infantry available owing to Brigade Reliefs.	Sap. Cannell wounded by Shrapnel in communication trench
30/6/15	—	Nos 1 & 2 Sections paraded 6.45 p.m. Met infantry working parties at SALLYPORT, YPRES at 9.15 p.m. & worked on communication trenches with 300 men of Infantry. 100 men Infantry carried up trench boards, & materials of all kinds for dugouts.	2 Infy. Killed, 3 " wounded by Shrapnel at École whilst marched [illegible]

[illegible] Capt. R.E. for MAJOR R.E. 1st FIELD Co. R.E.

1247 W 3299 200,000 (E) 8/14 J.B.C. & A. Forms/C. 2118/11.

14th Division

121/6357

61st F.C. R.E.

Vol: III

July 15

Instructions regarding War Diaries and Intelligence Summaries are contained in F. S. Regs., Part II. and the Staff Manual respectively. Title pages will be prepared in manuscript.

WAR DIARY
or
~~INTELLIGENCE SUMMARY.~~
(Erase heading not required.)

Army Form C. 2118.

Place	Date	Hour	Summary of Events and Information	Remarks and references to Appendices
	20/6/15		~~Nos 1 & 2 Sections paraded 6.45 pm Met infantry working parties at SALLYPORT YPRES at 9.15 PM & worked on comm trenches with 300 men of Infantry. 100 men Infantry carried up trench boards & materials of all kinds for dug outs.~~	~~2 Infy Killed 5 wounded [illegible]~~
H.7A.1.4.	1/7/15		Nos 3 & 4 Sections met working party of 400 men 5 R.S.Z.1. & worked on Communication & Assembly trenches. Communication trench I.17a.6.6 to I.11d.0.1. A carrying party of 100 men took up stores to BIRR x roads. 10 Sappers worked on dugouts at I.17 A 5.6.	2 men Killed & 2 wounded from the carrying party by shrapnel
"	2/7/15		Nos 1 & 2 Sections met working party at LILLE GATE, YPRES, met infantry party of 350 men & worked on communication & assembly trenches as for previous day. 50 men infantry & 10 sappers worked on dug outs I.17 A 5.6. 100 infantry carried up stores, wire, boards, sandbags etc, to BIRR x roads.	
"	3/7/15		Nos 3 & 4 Sections met working parties at LILLE GATE, YPRES. 400 with No 3 Section worked on assembly trenches in the neighborhood of WITTE POORT FARM. 250 with No 4 Section of communication trench Y. 50 men with some sappers worked on dug outs for Brigadier. Carrying party of 100 men carried Trench stores to BIRR x roads.	
"	4/7/15		Nos 1 & 2 sections proceeded to work. No 1 on assembly trenches round WITTE POORT farm, No 2 on dug outs for Brigadier. Infantry working parties were very late & only arrived on work at 12 midnight so that little work could be done.	

1577 Wt. W10791/1773 500,000 1/15 D. D. & L. A.D.S.S./Forms/C. 2118.

Army Form C. 2118.

Instructions regarding War Diaries and Intelligence Summaries are contained in F. S. Regs., Part II. and the Staff Manual respectively. Title pages will be prepared in manuscript.

WAR DIARY
or
~~INTELLIGENCE SUMMARY.~~

(Erase heading not required.)

Place	Date	Hour	Summary of Events and Information	Remarks and references to Appendices
H.7.A.1.4	5/7/15		Company took on duties in the front line trenches. Nos 3 & 4 Sections worked on same, repairing parapets etc, & making dugouts. Lt. Garrett Smith & Jenkins remained ~~out~~ in the trenches with their NCOs. 7 Saps were proceeded with by infantry under RE supervision.	
	6/7/15		No 1 & 2 Sections worked on front line repairing parapets etc, line was very unquiet & in some portions garrison stood to for 4 hours at a time. 7 Saps proceeded day & night.	9
	7/7/15		No 3 & 4 sections went up & spent 24 hours in Trenches. Trench extended 90x from 12 to 10. New trench behind 7 & 8 begun for 90x. Battalion dugouts commenced behind trench 7. Saps proceeded with day & night.	
	8.7.15		Nos 1 & 2 Sections went up to spend 48 hours in Trenches. Knife rests were constructed behind Railway wood, & some wire was placed in front of Trenches 12-10/4 & 3 working South. Progress was made in Saps.	
	9.7.15		Nos 1 & 2 Sections continued in trenches. Trench connecting 10 & 12 was completed through & some wire was placed in front of it, chiefly knife rests. Wire continued in front of 4, & apron form. Knife rests prepared. Saps proceeding satisfactorily. Sappers Swadling, Marley & Bruns (slightly) wounded 9.30 pm.	

Instructions regarding War Diaries and Intelligence Summaries are contained in F. S. Regs., Part II. and the Staff Manual respectively. Title pages will be prepared in manuscript.

WAR DIARY
or
~~INTELLIGENCE SUMMARY.~~

(*Erase heading not required.*)

Army Form C. 2118.

Place	Date	Hour	Summary of Events and Information	Remarks and references to Appendices
	10.7.15		Nos 3 & 4 Sections went into Front Line Trenches for 72 hours living at F1 and S13. Improved Trench connecting 10 & 12. Placing of wire in front of that & other front line trenches being proceeded with by 1, 2, & 5. Saps all proceeding fast & satisfactorily. One supporting point commenced in Railway Wood. Cpl Eldridge, Sprs Goddard & Pio Lawone & Spr Graham slightly wounded, 8.30pm	
	11.7.15		Nos 3 & 4 Sections in Trenches. Saps progressed very well. Wire carried all along. Completed loop in rear of 8 and No 7. Supporting Points, one in South of Railway Wood nearly completed & one in N of Railway Wood laid out, and one about I 17 b. 7.5 also laid out. Brigadier very pleased with progress in Sapping which have now average length of about 35 ft. ~~Spr Graham slightly wounded~~	
	12.7.15		Nos 3 & 4 Sections still in trenches. Wiring proceeded day & night. South supporting point Railway Wood continued. Supporting Point I 17 B 7.5 commenced.	
	13.7.15		Nos 1 & 2 relieved Nos 3 & 4 Sections in trenches. South Supporting Point Railway Wood nearly completed. Wiring continued. Trench 12 to 10 completed & occupied. Corporal Proctor and Sapper Miller wounded.	
	14.7.15		Nos 1 & 2 in trenches. Supporting Point N of Railway Wood begun, S of Railway Wood continued. Sap cut through from 9 to 7/8 and that from 7/8 to 6 approaching completion. Wiring continued. Spr Shields & Pioneer Truelove wounded.	

1577 Wt. W10791/1773 500,000 1/15 D. D. & L. A.D.S.S./Forms/C. 2118.

Instructions regarding War Diaries and Intelligence Summaries are contained in F. S. Regs., Part II. and the Staff Manual respectively. Title pages will be prepared in manuscript.

WAR DIARY
or
~~INTELLIGENCE SUMMARY.~~
(Erase heading not required.)

Army Form C. 2118.

Place	Date	Hour	Summary of Events and Information	Remarks and references to Appendices
15.7.15			No 1 & 2 Sections relieved in afternoon by 63rd Co RE, 4 NCOs & 16 men were sent back early to supervise work on 16th. Laid out defences S of Menin Road near White Chateau. No 3 Section & 300 infantry worked on supporting point behind White Chateau ~~[illegible]~~ during night.	
16.7.15			300 infantry employed under supervision of a few parties of Nos 1 & 2 Sections & Maj Mackesy, Capt Cheney, CSM Bayes on supporting points about 1 mile SE of VLAMERTINGHE. No 4 Sec supervised 300 infantry who owing to rain only arrived at works 11.30pm & stopped at 1.30am and by order I Corps Comdr had to start on points in front of White Chateau which had not been laid out.	[illegible]
~~17.7.15~~ 17.7.15			No 1 & 2 Sections with 2 reliefs each of 300 infantry worked on Rear supporting Points near I.10.c & I.16. No 3 Section with 300 infantry worked at night on supporting point in front of WHITECHATEAU ~~[illegible]~~ but owing to non arrival of motors work could not be laid out in daylight.	
18.7.15			Sappers of Nos 1 & 2 worked on front Points about I.10.c & I.16. No infantry owing to relief. No 4 Section & 400 infantry worked at night on supporting points in front of Chateau which were laid out at dusk by Major Mackesy	
19.7.15			Sappers of Nos 1 & 2 sections with in afternoon 400 infantry worked on Supporting Points I.10.c & I.16. No 3 Section & 400 infantry worked by night on defences in front of White Chateau	
20.7.15			Nos 1 & 2 sections with 2 reliefs each of 400 infantry worked on Supporting Points I.10.c & I.16. No 4 Sect. with 400 infantry worked on defences in front of Chateau 11pm to 12.30am. Owing to heavy shelling infantry were unable to get beyond YPRES until after 10pm hence delay in starting work	

1577 Wt. W10791/1773 500,000 1/15 D. D. & L. A.D.S.S./Forms/C. 2118.

Instructions regarding War Diaries and Intelligence Summaries are contained in F. S. Regs., Part II. and the Staff Manual respectively. Title pages will be prepared in manuscript.

WAR DIARY
or
~~INTELLIGENCE SUMMARY.~~

(*Erase heading not required.*)

Army Form C. 2118.

Place	Date	Hour	Summary of Events and Information	Remarks and references to Appendices
			Shewed OC 89 F[ield] Co. round supporting works at H10 & H16 & in front of Chateau which he is taking over from tomorrow 21st inclusive via 61st Co. going to trenches with 14th Inf Bde.	
21.7.15			Company rested. Capt Chesney shewn round trenches by Officer of 56th Field Co. Lt Gordon.	
22.7.15			Company practised at laying out traces of traversed & zig zag trenches and in bomb making. Capt Chesney Lts Paddison & Birchell went round trenches	
23.7.15			Nos 1 & 2 sections went up to trenches sapping in dugouts at SANCTUARY WOOD. Work done as under during night 10 Sappers with 70 infantry at gap between C1 & C2, 8 men with Inf at CRATER, 6 men at cuts in MENIN Road from C10 also at Sap to Y wood. No 3 Section & 1 Coy Pioneers undertook Comm Trench at about I 16 a 3.0 to G.H.Q. 2nd Line. Major Mackenzy. Lt. Sankey visited trenches.	
24.7.15			Nos 1 & 2 sections continued cuts in the MENIN ROAD, cleared TUNNEL HOUSE, repaired parapets in C_5, C_2 & STRAND. A certain amount of work done on T heads in S_3a, making knife rests, & on saps at C.10. No 4 Section worked at night on communication trench at G.H.Q 2nd Line. Sapper W. McGowan wounded.	
25.7.15			Nos 1 & 2 Sections in trenches, continued cuts in the MENIN ROAD, parapets of fire trenches, trench already dug cleared & roadway STRAND repaired. Retrenchment behind stables, laid out & continued as sap. Communication trenches laid out, (1) from NEW BOND ST. to OXFORD ST (2) from STRAND to S_2 (3) from S_2 to trench in SANCTUARY WOOD. Major Mackenzy, Lt Garrett Smith & Sergt Watson inspected sites for G.H.Q. dugouts & ZILLEBEKE dressing station Sapper Doyle killed	

1577 Wt. W10791/1773 500,000 1/15 D. D. & L. A.D.S.S./Forms/C. 2118.

Instructions regarding War Diaries and Intelligence Summaries are contained in F. S. Regs., Part II. and the Staff Manual respectively. Title pages will be prepared in manuscript.

WAR DIARY

or

~~INTELLIGENCE SUMMARY.~~

(Erase heading not required.)

Place	Date	Hour	Summary of Events and Information	Remarks and references to Appendices
25.7.15 (contd)			No 3 section worked at night under Cpl Coyde & completed loop. No 4 Section trench stores.	
26.7.15.			Nos 1 & 2 section in trenches continued MENIN ROAD cut, repaired STRAND, worked on T heads in S_3a. Dugouts for G.H.Q. laid out by Sergt Watson. 3 & 4 section trench stores. Lt. Fenwick joined the Co.	
27.7.15.			Nos 1 & 2 section in trenches continued MENIN ROAD cuts, general repairing of trenches & trench stores. 3 & 4 sections relieved 1 & 2 in trenches at night. Stores for dressing station at ZILLEBEKE. Major Markey showed Lt Fenwick round trenches. No 3 & 4 Sections cleared TUNNEL HOUSE, continued trench behind STABLES & repaired G.1	
28.7.15			Nos 3 & 4 Sections in trenches repaired STRAND, BOND ST & worked in S_3a, Saps 1.2.3 & 4.6 restarted, communication trench from BOND ST to new line of OXFORD ST marked out, retrenchment behind STABLES repaired, trench along N. edge SANCTUARY WOOD converted into fire trench & commun. trench laid out by Lt Garnett Smith from this to connect up with S_2 wiring G_1 G_2 continued. Switch communication off OXFORD ST. laid out by Lt Fenwick. SALLY PORT in repair & collect casks at night. 3 Saps detailed to keep pontoon bridge by SALLY PORT in repair & collect casks at night for barrel pier	
29.7.15.			Nos 3 & 4 section in trenches continued working at saps & repair of trenches Spr Palliser wounded. No 2 Section worked at night on trenches in G.H.Q. 2nd Line.	
30.7.15			Nos 3 & 4 section in trenches enemy attacked position at HOOGE using liquid fire, & captured several trenches, Lt Garnett-Smith & party (bombing party &) helped & improved trenches still retained, G_1 & S_2 Lt Jenks	

Army Form C. 2118.

Instructions regarding War Diaries and Intelligence Summaries are contained in F. S. Regs., Part II. and the Staff Manual respectively. Title pages will be prepared in manuscript.

WAR DIARY

or

~~INTELLIGENCE SUMMARY.~~

(Erase heading not required.)

Place	Date	Hour	Summary of Events and Information	Remarks and references to Appendices
30. 7. 15			with small party helped make up bombs. & removed bomb store which was in danger of being captured. Lt Garnett Smith was severely wounded. Spr Redmond killed Sprs. Stellin, Campbell & Spencer wounded. Later employed in making knife rests	
			Nos 1 & 2 section with all officers went to ramparts YPRES during counter attack ~~at~~ & left there for trenches at 8.30 p.m. assisted infantry to deepen S_{3a}, ~~S_3~~ & S_4, also made M. G. emplacements in S_4 & S_3 till stopped by bombardment early 31.7.15. & wiring between ZOUAVE & SANCT. WOODS.	
31. 7. 15			~~[illegible]~~ All 4 sections in trenches, heavy bombardment. Wounded Cpls. Arnold Oldridge & Cozola. Sprs. Allen Cherry, Kirk, Ladbroke, McElveny, O'Connell, Durnant & Allan Missing Sprs Lawrence & Townsin. No work possible, assisted stretcher bearers, & repaired 2 M.G. emplacements in rear of ZOUAVE WOOD.	
1. 8. 15			4 section in trenches. Made knife rests, improved S_{3a} support trench laid out by Lt Birkett in rear of ZOUAVE WOOD, made up bombs, helped stretcher bearers. Lt Paddison wounded.	
			Major Mackesy appointed a/CRE. XIV Divn. 61st Co. taken over by Lt. Fenwick	
			Capt. Benskin Cmdg. 89th Fd Co. took over work in trenches & was shown round by Lt Birkett.	
			3 & 4 sections returned to camp at night.	
2. 8. 15			Nos 1 & 2 section returned in morning. Co. rested in camp.	

14th Division

K

121/6754

61st F.C.R.E.

Vol: IV

August 15

Instructions regarding War Diaries and Intelligence Summaries are contained in F. S. Regs., Part II. and the Staff Manual respectively. Title pages will be prepared in manuscript.

61st Fd Co RE
XIV Div

WAR DIARY
or
INTELLIGENCE SUMMARY.
(Erase heading not required.)

Army Form C. 2118.

Place	Date	Hour	Summary of Events and Information	Remarks and references to Appendices
Hqa.	1/8/15		4 Sections in trenches. Made knife rests; improved S 3a; support trench laid out by Lt Buckell in rear of ZOUAVE WOOD, made up bombs, helped stretcher bearers. Lt Paddison wounded. Major Mackenzie appointed a/C.R.E. XIV Div. 61st Co taken over by Lt. Fenwick. Capt Benskin comdg. 89 Fd Co took over work in trenches and was shewn round by Lt Buckell. 3 & 4 Sections returned to camp at night.	
	2/8/15		Nos 1 & 2 Sections returned in morning. 3 & 4 rested in camp.	
	3/8/15		No 3 Constructed Bridge for Transport on earth road North of ZILLEBEKE Lake. No 4 Sec worked on dugouts ~~at [illegible]~~ OXFORD STREET and Shelter for stretcher cases ZILLEBEKE. Nos 1 & 2 on camp work.	
	4/8/15		No 1 Sec constructed Barrel Piers for repair Pontoon Bridge YPRES. No 2 Sec on dressing Station ZILLEBEKE. Nos 3 & 4 Sec on work in Camp. Lt Temperley joined. Lt Col Biggs arrived 5pm as CRE & Major Mackenzie rejoined Co.	
	5/8/15		Completed Girder Bridge for Transport & continued work on Dressing Station. Lt Rowley joined Co & he and Lt Fenwick started taking over Nos 3 & 1 Sections respectively.	
	6/8/15		No 4 Sec at Dressing Station. Others ready for night work but stopped on account of Bombardment & no infantry parties available. Practised laying out Traces & camp work.	
	7/8/15		Draft of 28 men joined Coy. Pontoon Bridge repaired. Dressing Station completed. Sections reformed with new Draft. Collected materials from YPRES. Started work on rear supporting Point	

1577 Wt. W10791/1773 500,000 1/15 D. D. & L. A.D.S.S./Forms/C. 2118.

61st Field Coy RE
XIV Div.

Instructions regarding War Diaries and Intelligence Summaries are contained in F. S. Regs., Part II. and the Staff Manual respectively. Title pages will be prepared in manuscript.

WAR DIARY
or
INTELLIGENCE SUMMARY.
(Erase heading not required.)

Army Form C. 2118.

Place	Date	Hour	Summary of Events and Information	Remarks and references to Appendices
8/8/15			Nos 1 & 2 Sections started erecting Huts Divl Headquarters. No 3 & 4 Section worked on 4 Rear Supporting Points H10 & H16, with infantry parties of 400 men in 2 reliefs of 4 hours each.	
9/8/15			Work as 8th. Cpl Whitby killed by a shell at YORKSHIRE Redoubt.	
10/8/15			Work as 8th.	
11/8/15			Work on 4 supporting Points, Divisional Huts & Dugout for CRE	
12/8/15			Work as 11th	
13/8/15			Nos 1 & 2 Sections left in afternoon to cellars in N of YPRES to work in front trenches of 'A' Sector. During night No 1 Sect moved into Dugouts vacated by 56th Field Co at KAAIE. No 4 section working on Huts. No 3 on CRE's dugout & roads. Lt Fenwick sick & 2/Lt Tempurley took charge of No 1 Sec.	
14/8/15			Nos 1 & 2 Sections on trenches. No 1 Section worked on Communication Trench N of Railway Wood & on machine gun emplacement in A2. No 2 worked on Communications to OBER Houses & Heel Street. Nos 3 & 4 Sections as on 13th.	
[illegible]			No 2 Section moved from cellars of Convent in afternoon to strengthen cellars in Petroleum Depot at KAAIE YPRES.	

1577 Wt. W10791/1773 500,000 1/15 D. D. & L. A.D.S.S./Forms/C. 2118.

Instructions regarding War Diaries and Intelligence Summaries are contained in F. S. Regs., Part II. and the Staff Manual respectively. Title pages will be prepared in manuscript.

WAR DIARY
or
INTELLIGENCE SUMMARY.
(Erase heading not required.)

Army Form C. 2118.

Place	Date	Hour	Summary of Events and Information	Remarks and references to Appendices
15/8/15			Nos. 1 & 2 sections – Trenches. Worked on POTIJZE defences, revetting Strand and Cheapside. Improved Commn. trench WOOD Houses & completed M.G. Emplacement – A2. Started clean Bellewaarde Beek. Sappers Steele & Sinclair wounded. No 3 Roads, No 4 Section completed huts. Made hurdles & dugout frames – Camp.	
16/8/15			Nos 1 & 2 in Trenches worked on Communication Trenches. defences of POTIJZE. Laid land mine at OOSTER Houses. Made Bomb store in X5. Repaired trench boards. Supervised Infantry on WARWICK LINES, & continued clearing of Bellewaarde Beek.	
17/8/15			Nos 3 & 4 sections relieved Nos 1 & 2 in trenches in late afternoon. Work done. Commn. Trench near POTIJZE continued also WARWICK LINES & Commn Trench South of Piccadilly	
18/8/15			Nos 1 & 2 sections on roads – morning for a couple of hours then to Baths at Poperinghe. Nos 3 & 4 commenced M.G. emplacement – A3, worked with 5th KRR in the trenches – I 11 a at night, commenced drainage Haymarket by day & work on Warwick lines & on trench WOOD Houses by night. Sapper J. Campbell wounded.	
19/8/15			Much the same as on 18/8/15 –	

1577 Wt. W10791/1773 500,000 1/15 D. D. & L. A.D.S.S./Forms/C. 2118.

Instructions regarding War Diaries and Intelligence Summaries are contained in F. S. Regs., Part II. and the Staff Manual respectively. Title pages will be prepared in manuscript.

WAR DIARY
or
INTELLIGENCE SUMMARY.
(Erase heading not required.)

Army Form C. 2118.

Place	Date	Hour	Summary of Events and Information	Remarks and references to Appendices
20/8/15.			No 1 Section on roads, No 2 on Huts & dugouts. No 3 Section on Front trench & Comm. trench off Piccadilly. No 4 OBER House & WARWICK LINES & STRAND. Nos 3 & 4 being in front trenches.	
21/8/15.			Nos 3 & 4 started Dugouts KAAIE Salient for Brigade Headquarters and Battalion Headquarters. Other work same as 19th.	
22/8/15.			Nos 3 & 4 in Trenches. Dugouts in Kaaie Salient in daytime & Machine Gun Emplacements in X2 X4 & X5. Nos 1 & 2 as before. Piccadilly Switch in evening.	
23/8/15.			3 & 4 Sections KAAIE Dugouts. Relieved by 1 & 2 sections in evening. No 1 Piccadilly Switch & MG Empl. – X1. No 2 MG Empls – X4.	
24/8/15 – 28/8/15			Nos 1 & 2 in trenches. Worked on Kaaie Salient by day on dugouts for Brigade HQrs & Reserve Battn. HQrs. By night on Piccadilly Switch, Piccadilly & Haymarket. Part No 4 on Bde Dugouts by day, remainder Camp work. No 3 on roads.	
29/8/15.			Nos 3 & 4 relieved Nos 1 & 2 Sections in Trenches. Party of 10 men No 2 remained with them on Bt HQrs Dugouts by day.	
30/8/15 – 31/8/15			Dugouts by day. By night clearing BELLEWAARDE BEEK & within Piccadilly O.T. & work on Haymarket. Wiring in front of A4 & MG Empls in A4 & in X1. No 2 (balance) on roads, No 1 on Shelters & Camp work.	

1577 Wt. W10791/1773 500,000 1/15 D. D. & L. A.D.S.S./Forms/C. 2118.

14th Division

121
6992

61st F.C.R.E.
Vol: V

Sept. 15

61st Field Coy. R.E.

WAR DIARY
or
INTELLIGENCE SUMMARY.

(*Erase heading not required.*)

Army Form C. 2118.

September 1915.

Instructions regarding War Diaries and Intelligence Summaries are contained in F. S. Regs., Part II. and the Staff Manual respectively. Title pages will be prepared in manuscript.

Place	Date	Hour	Summary of Events and Information	Remarks and references to Appendices
H Q a	1st		Nos 3 & 4 Sections in Trenches NE of YPRES. Bn't working on Brigade HQrs & Battalion HQrs. Dugouts at KAAIE by day & revetting & draining Comm. Trenches & clearing BELLEWARDE BEEK & working on PICCADILLY [illegible] & M.G. Emplacements & dugouts – front line (A4) &c.	
			Nos 1 & 2 Sections – Camp on Roads, Hurdles, Huts etc.	
"	2		Nos 3 & 4 on Bde & Bn HQrs dugouts by day. Nos 1 & 2 in Camp moving [illegible]. } Heavy rain no Infantry Parties.	
"	3		Much the same as 2nd.	
"	4		Nos 3 & 4 at Dugouts – daytime & then back to Camp on relief by Nos 1 & 2 to Front Trenches.	
"	5		Nos 1 & 2 in Trenches revetting and sandbagging PICCADILLY, HAYMARKET comm trenches and building dugouts at KAAIE. Left Half Company resting	
"	6		Nos 1 & 2 draining front line and comm trenches, and working on Battalion dugouts. Nos 3 & 4 re-roofed section dugouts in camp.	
"	7		Nos 1 & 2 clearing BELLEWAARDE BEEK and other drainage. Nos 3 & 4 making hurdles and other stores in Company workshop.	

1577 Wt. W10791/1773 500,000 1/15 D. D. & L. A.D.S.S./Forms/C. 2118.

Instructions regarding War Diaries and Intelligence Summaries are contained in F. S. Regs., Part II. and the Staff Manual respectively. Title pages will be prepared in manuscript.

WAR DIARY of 61st Field Co. R.E.
or
~~INTELLIGENCE SUMMARY.~~
(Erase heading not required.)

September 1915

Army Form C. 2118.

Place	Date	Hour	Summary of Events and Information	Remarks and references to Appendices
H.2a.33	8		Nos 1 2+3 Sections as on day before. No 4 section and 4 wagon getting timber from YPRES.	
	9		Company as on 7th.	
	10		Nos 1+2 worked on KAAIE dugouts till relieved by Left Half Company, who then worked on drainage.	
	11		Nos 3+4 Sections in trenches, revetting commn trenches, and commenced a new switch to HAYMARKET; also proceeded with dugouts. Remainder of Company rested	
	12		Nos 3+4 continued dugouts and worked on commn trenches Nos 1+2 repaired Section dugouts in camp.	
	13		Company as on 12th.	
	14		Nos 3+4 at work in trenches as before. Nos 1+2 made hurdles, pickets etc in Co workshop.	
	15		Nos 3+4 finished new SWITCH to HAYMARKET + continued on other commns. Timber was obtained from YPRES by No 1 Section, while No 2 continued in workshop.	

1577 Wt. W10791/1773 500,000 1/15 D. D. & L. A.D.S.S./Forms/C. 2118.

Instructions regarding War Diaries and Intelligence Summaries are contained in F. S. Regs., Part II. and the Staff Manual respectively. Title pages will be prepared in manuscript.

WAR DIARY or ~~INTELLIGENCE SUMMARY.~~ 61st Field Co. R.E.

(Erase heading not required.)

September 1915

Army Form C. 2118.

Place	Date	Hour	Summary of Events and Information	Remarks and references to Appendices
H7a 33	16		Nos 3 + 4 continued dugouts at KAAIE. Nos 1+2 made loophole boxes in camp, and then relieved Nos 3+4 in trenches.	
	17th		Nos 1+2 sections worked on drainage of HAYMARKET, PICCADILLY and other communications, also continued work on Dugouts in KAAIE SALIENT. Nos 3+4 sections rested.	
	18th		Nos 1+2 sections as on 17th. Nos 3+4 sections made trench stores in Co. workshops and worked on Roads	
	19th		Company at work as on 18th. Sapper W. Pallister wounded at POTIJZE Dump	
	20th		Work as before	
	21st		As before. II Cpl Barnes & Sapper Seale wounded at KAAIE dugouts; Seale died in hospital.	
	22nd		Nos 1+2 Sections continued drainage of commn. trenches + worked on dugouts; No 3 collected timber etc. from YPRES. No 4 worked on ditches near camp.	
	23rd		Nos 1+2 Sections were relieved by Nos 3+4 Sections in morning, who then continued work in the drainage of commn trenches.	
	24th		No 3 Section worked on CANAL Dugouts and No 4 Section on drainage. Right Half Company at work in Company Workshop.	
	25th		No 3 + 4 Sections cleaning dugouts at KAAIE owing to bombardment. Nos 1+2 in camp and in company workshop.	

1577 Wt. W10791/1773 500,000 1/15 D. D. & L. A.D.S.S./Forms/C. 2118.

Instructions regarding War Diaries and Intelligence Summaries are contained in F. S. Regs., Part II. and the Staff Manual respectively. Title pages will be prepared in manuscript.

WAR DIARY
or
~~INTELLIGENCE~~ SUMMARY.
(Erase heading not required.)

of 61st Field Co. R.E.
September 1915.

Army Form C. 2118.

Place	Date	Hour	Summary of Events and Information	Remarks and references to Appendices
H.13.a.3.3	26th		Nos 3 & 4 improving KRAIE dugouts and making trench stores.	
			Nos 1 & 2 as before	
	27th		Left Half Company draining and revetting communication trenches	
			Right Half Company as before	
	28th		Company as on 27th	
	29th		Nos 3 & 4 sections as on 27th. Very heavy rain.	
			No 1 began permanent work on Huts under Lt. TEMPERLEY. No 2 collecting timbers and bricks from YPRES & VLAMERTINGHE	
	30th		No 3 Section at work on CANAL dugouts till relieved by No 2 section in afternoon	
			No 4 Section continued drainage of HAYMARKET & adjacent trenches.	
			No 1 Section continued huts.	

1577 Wt. W10791/1773 500,000 1/15 D. D. & L. A.D.S.S./Forms/C. 2118.

14th Division

121/743 Y

61st F.C. R.E.
Vol: 6

Oct 15

Instructions regarding War Diaries and Intelligence Summaries are contained in F. S. Regs., Part II. and the Staff Manual respectively. Title pages will be prepared in manuscript.

61st Field Coy R.E.

WAR DIARY
or
~~INTELLIGENCE SUMMARY.~~
(Erase heading not required.)

October 1915

Army Form C. 2118.

Place	Date	Hour	Summary of Events and Information	Remarks and references to Appendices
H,a 33	1/10		No 2 Section at work on KAAIE dugouts and drainage of PICCADILLY. No 4 Section continued repair and drainage of HAYMARKET. No 1 Section on Hutting + No 3 on general camp work	
	2/10		as on 1st. No 4 section returned to camp.	
	3/10		No 2 Section in trenches ~~at work~~ on PICCADILLY + HAYMARKET commns. No 1 Section Hutting. Nos 3+4 sections making trench stores in Company workshop and on roads.	
	4/10		No 2 in trenches working on communications; No 3 went up to trenches in afternoon + worked on MENIN ROAD Dump. No 1 Section Hutting; No 4 Section training class of infantry from 41st Bde in Field Works.	
	5/10		As on 4th.	
	6/10		Nos 2+3 sections making knife rests and collecting stores at KAAIE. Nos 1+4 section as on 4th.	
	7/10		No 2 Section making M.G. Emplt in X1; No 3 Section placing knife rests in H19. Rest of Company as on 4th	
	8/10		Same as on 7th	
	9/10		No 2 Section continuing M.G. Emplt in X1 + began new cutting for MUDDY LANE; No 3 wiring in H14 + H5. Rest of Company as before	
	10/10		As on 9th. Lt Dinwick from Adjutant 14th Div Corps came to command No 4 Sahin 61 Co in place of Lt Leeks who became Adjutant – hospital	

1577 Wt. W10791/1773 500,000 1/15 D. D. & L. A.D.S.S./Forms/C. 2118.

Instructions regarding War Diaries and Intelligence Summaries are contained in F. S. Regs., Part II. and the Staff Manual respectively. Title pages will be prepared in manuscript.

61st Field Co R.E.

WAR DIARY
or
INTELLIGENCE SUMMARY.

(Erase heading not required.)

October 1915

Army Form C. 2118.

Place	Date	Hour	Summary of Events and Information	Remarks and references to Appendices
H7a 33	11/10		No 2 Section wiring R 4; No 3 section making knife rests and fixing them at H14. No 1 Section hutting; No 4 Section making trench stores etc in Co. Workshop.	
	12/10		As on 11th.	
	13/10		No 2 + 3 making knife rests + working on dugouts at KEMMEL till relieved by No 4 Section. No 1 Section hutting; details made knife rests and horse troughs in Workshop	
	14/10		No 4 Section doing general work in HAYMARKET + PICCADILLY communication trenches. Nos 2 + 3 sections rested, No 1 Section hutting	
	15/10		No 4 Section continued work on communication trenches and wiring S.8. Joined by Lt. CROFTON and part of No 1 Section for work on WHITE CHATEAU and YPRES defences. Nos 2 + 3 sections doing camp work and preparing stores for front line. Rest of No 1 Hutting.	
	16/10		No 1 Section as before; No 4 Section as on 15th. No 2 Section instructing Infantry Class + preparing stores, No 3 Section general Camp Work.	
	17/10		No 4 Section working on commun. trenches, then putting new mine crater at H20 in a state of defence. Rest of Company as on 16th.	
	18/10		No 4 Section clearing new trenches round mine crater, Rest of Company as on 16th.	

1577 Wt. W10791/1773 500,000 1/15 D. D. & L. A.D.S.S./Forms/C. 2118.

Instructions regarding War Diaries and Intelligence Summaries are contained in F. S. Regs., Part II. and the Staff Manual respectively. Title pages will be prepared in manuscript.

61st Field Co. R.E.

WAR DIARY
or
~~INTELLIGENCE SUMMARY.~~
(Erase heading not required.)

October 1915

Army Form C. 2118.

Place	Date	Hour	Summary of Events and Information	Remarks and references to Appendices
	19/10/15		No 4 Section continued work round new mine crater and S20 Rest of Company as on 16th	
	20/10/15		No 4 Section working on drainage of communication trenches, Rest of Company as on 16th	
	21/10/15		No 4 Section clearing HAYMARKET which had been flooded; Remainder as before	
	22/10/15		as on 21st; No 4 Section and part of No 1 Section returned to camp	
	23/10/15		No 1 Section Hutting; No 3 Section working on Camp Buildings; No 2 & 4 Section rested	
	24/10/15		as on 23rd	
	25–31/10/15		Company engaged in Hutting and Military training	
			[signature] Major RE OC 61 Coy 31/10/15	

14th Division

61st F.C.R.E.
Vol 7

121/7658

Nov. 15.

61st Field Company R.E.

Instructions regarding War Diaries and Intelligence Summaries are contained in F. S. Regs., Part II. and the Staff Manual respectively. Title pages will be prepared in manuscript.

WAR DIARY
or
~~INTELLIGENCE SUMMARY~~
(Erase heading not required.)

November 1915

Army Form C. 2118.

Hour, Date, Place	Summary of Events and Information	Remarks and references to Appendices
1st + 2nd. HQa.	No 1 Section working in Divisional Hutting Factory; No 3 Section building Company huts; Nos 2+4 Sections making trench stores etc.	
3rd	No 1 Section Hutting; No 2 Section Company hutting; Nos 3+4 making trench stores	
4th – 8th	Nos 1+3 Sections Divisional Hutting; No 2 Section Company Hutting; No 4 Section building specimen German trenches and making trench stores	
9th – 13th	No 1 Section hutting; No 2 Section Company hutting; No 3 Section making hurdles; No 4 Section continued German type trenches and instruction party of Infantry in field defences	
14th	No 1 Section hutting; Nos 2+3 Sections loading + unloading stores for Instructional Breastworks for 41st Inf Bde; No 4 as before.	
15th – 16th	No 1 as before; No 2 Company hutting; No 3 instructing Inf in Breastworks etc; No 4 in German trenches and Instruction class.	
17th	Nos 1, 2+4 as before. No 3 making trenches stores. Officers of 61st Field Co shown over trenches in new sector by 1st London Fd Co. RE (T.F.) taking over their trenches on conclusion of Rest Period	
18th	No 1 on hutting; No 4 trench stores; No 2 Section (Lt BUCKELL) + No 3 Section (Lt ROWLEY) under Major MACKESY went up to dugouts on Canal Bank at C25c, on taking over trenches from 1st London Fd Co. (6th Division)	

61st Field Company R.E

WAR DIARY
or
~~INTELLIGENCE SUMMARY~~
(Erase heading not required.)

Army Form C. 2118.

November 1915

Instructions regarding War Diaries and Intelligence Summaries are contained in F. S. Regs., Part II. and the Staff Manual respectively. Title pages will be prepared in manuscript.

Hour, Date, Place	Summary of Events and Information	Remarks and references to Appendices
19th	Nos 2+3 sections in Front trenches about C21 (Sheet 28), and working on dugouts on CANAL BANK at C25c. No1 Section Hutting & No4 making trench stores in camp.	
20th	No2+3 commenced breastworks near MARK LANE + B14; continued CANAL dugouts. Nos 1+4 sections as before	
21st	No2+3 sections with infantry worked on drainage of WILLOW WALK, DUNLOP STREET, S18, S14; continued MARK LANE Breastworks and CANAL dugouts No1 Hutting, No4 rested.	
22nd	Nos 2+3 continued drainage of communication and support trenches; worked on repair of tramway and CANAL Dugouts. No1 part Hutting & part trench stores. No4 part Company Hutting & part trench stores	
23rd	Front line sections continued draining front and support trenches and CANAL dugouts; Sappers [illegible] and Goddard wounded Work in camp as before.	
24th	Front line sections on drainage of front and support trenches, and erecting dugouts on CANAL Bank. Work in camp as before	
25th	No2 Section draining CORNHILL, erecting Breastworks and dugouts on CANAL BANK. No3 Section draining front and support trenches, and wiring S16B. No1 & 4 as before.	

1247 W 3299 200,000 (E) 8/14 J.B.C. & A. Forms/C. 2118/11.

Instructions regarding War Diaries and Intelligence Summaries are contained in F. S. Regs., Part II. and the Staff Manual respectively. Title pages will be prepared in manuscript.

61st Field Co. R.E XIV Div

WAR DIARY

or

~~INTELLIGENCE SUMMARY~~

(Erase heading not required.)

Army Form C. 2118.

November 1915

Hour, Date, Place	Summary of Events and Information	Remarks and references to Appendices
26/11/15	No 2 section repairing Bridges over CANAL + continuing dugouts; No 3 Section returned to camp being relieved by No 1 Section; Cpl Collins + Pioneer Shimmin wounded. No 4 section worked on Trench stores.	
27/11/15	No 1 Section draining and wiring trenches around S16B; No 2 Section draining CORNHILL + S13C and working on Breastwork; 7 men of No 3 section remained on drainage and were joined by 6 more; remainder of section on trench stores; No 4 Section made trench stores	
28/11/15	No 1 Section working around S15B; No 2 Section drainage of CORNHILL and neighbouring trenches, also work on CANAL dugouts and repair of Trench Tramway; Part of No 3 section drainage in front line, rest of section with No 4 section made trench stores in camp.	
29/11/15	As on 28th;	
30/11/15	No 1 + 2 Sections working on Cornhill.	

[illegible] Major RE
O.C. 61 Coy R.E.
30/11/15

1247 W 3299 200,000 (E) 8/14 J.B.C. & A. Forms/C. 2118/11.

14 Div

61st F.C.R.E.

Vol: 8

Dec 1915

121/7936

61st Field Coy RE.
14th Division

Army Form C. 2118.

Instructions regarding War Diaries and Intelligence Summaries are contained in F. S. Regs., Part II. and the Staff Manual respectively. Title pages will be prepared in manuscript.

WAR DIARY
or
~~INTELLIGENCE SUMMARY~~

(Erase heading not required.)

December. 1915

Hour, Date, Place		Summary of Events and Information	Remarks and references to Appendices
Ha3.3.	1/12/15	No 1 Section at S16B erecting dummy breastwork and constructing aid post, and on drainage ~~S7~~ B16. No 2 Section working on CORNHILL. No 3 constructing dugouts on CANAL BANK. No 4 making trench stores in camp. relieved No 2 section in afternoon.	
	2nd.	Nos 1 & 3 Sections as on 1st. No 4 Section working on CORNHILL. No 2 Section making trench stores in camp.	
	3rd	As on 2nd. Lt. CROFTON went to hospital	
	4th	Nos 1 & ~~4~~ sections working on BREASTWORK and drainage of front trenches. No 4 working on CORNHILL & repairing trench tramway. Part of No 2 working on CANAL dugouts, remainder with No 3 section hutting and making trench stores in camp.	
	5th	Nos 1 + 4 Sections as before. No 2 Section Camp Roads, No 3 Section Trench Stores	
	6th	As on 5th	
	7th	No 1 Section laying and repairing trench tramway and draining BOUNDARY ROAD No 4 on CORNHILL. Nos 2 + 3 in camp as before.	
	8th	As on 7th.	

1247 W 3299 200,000 (E) 8/14 J.B.C. & A. Forms/C. 2118/11.

61st Field Coy. R.E.
14th Division

Instructions regarding War Diaries and Intelligence Summaries are contained in F. S. Regs., Part II. and the Staff Manual respectively. Title pages will be prepared in manuscript.

WAR DIARY
or
~~INTELLIGENCE SUMMARY~~
(Erase heading not required.)

December 1915

Army Form C. 2118.

Hour, Date, Place	Summary of Events and Information	Remarks and references to Appendices
9th	No 3 section relieved No 1 Section. 2/Lt. WILLMER joined Co. and took charge of No 1 Section. No 3 section on drainage of BOUNDARY ROAD + repairing TRAMWAY. No 4 " continued work on CORNHILL. No 2 section continued trench stores.	
10th.	Nos 2 3 + 4 as on 9th; No 1 Section worked on Camp Roads	
11th.	No 3 commenced dam in BOUNDARY ROAD DRAIN, Rest of Company as before.	
12th	As on 11th.	
13th + 14th	As on 11th.	
15th.	~~No.~~ No working parties for front line; Nos 3+4 section repaired trench tramway and worked on CANAL dugouts, work in camp as before	
16th	Front line sections to camp.	
17th - 25th	Company preparing to move; completing stores and equipment; repairing wagons and loading them; repairing camp roads; getting camp ready to hand over. Company stood to on morning of 19th owing to gas attack East of YPRES.	

1247 W 3299 200,000 (E) 8/14 J.B.C. & A. Forms/C. 2118/11.

Instructions regarding War Diaries and Intelligence Summaries are contained in F. S. Regs., Part II. and the Staff Manual respectively. Title pages will be prepared in manuscript.

61st Field Co RE
14th Division

WAR DIARY
or
~~INTELLIGENCE SUMMARY~~
(Erase heading not required.)

Army Form C. 2118.

December 1915.

Hour, Date, Place	Summary of Events and Information	Remarks and references to Appendices
25th	Christmas Day; order to stand to.	
26th	Orders to move postponed then cancelled.	
27th	Major MACKESY, Lt ROWLEY, 2nd Lt WILLMER went to reconnoitre trenches near BOESINGHE, on taking them over from 1st/2nd West Riding Field Co RE.	
28th	No 1 Section to trenches; No 2 section camp roads, No 3 Section Company Hutting. No 4 erecting huts in ELVERDINGHE WOOD.	
29th	No 1 Section improving dugouts; No 3 section working at night on C. Breastwork. No 2 + 4 erecting huts in ELVERDINGHE WOOD; heavy shelling.	
30th	No 1 Section improving dugouts, repairing Bridge + Tramway No 2 " working on trench stores and camp roads No 3 " working at night on C. Breastwork. No 4 Section hutting at ELVERDINGHE	
31st	As on 30th except No 3 did not go up to work at night.	

[signature]
MAJOR R.E.
O.C. 61st FIELD Co. R.E.

14th Div

Jan 1916

61st F.C.R.E.

Vol: 9

Instructions regarding War Diaries and Intelligence Summaries are contained in F. S. Regs., Part II. and the Staff Manual respectively. Title pages will be prepared in manuscript.

61st Field Co. RE 14th Division

WAR DIARY
or
~~INTELLIGENCE SUMMARY~~

(Erase heading not required.)

January 1916

Army Form C. 2118.

Hour, Date, Place	Summary of Events and Information	Remarks and references to Appendices
1st — 5th	No 1 Section on CANAL bank improving dugouts & repairing bridges; also at work on LANCASHIRE FARM Tramway	
	No 2 Section in camp making trench stoves and camp duties.	
	No 3 Section going up to work at night on "C" Breastwork then on Tramway	
	No 4 Section Divisional Hutting at ELVERDINGHE	
6th — 11th	No 1. Section go to new camp at A18d (sheet 28), and prepare it for occupation.	
	No 2 Section at CANAL bank, building dugouts, repairing Bridge 6 and ~~also laying~~ dismantling and loading engine & dynamo; also laying planking for tramway on LANCASHIRE FARM Tramway	
	No 3 Section Divisional Hutting at ELVERDINGHE	
	No 4 Section at work at night extending LANCASHIRE FARM Tramway, and wiring 'C' Breastwork.	
	Major MACKESY assumed Actg/C.R.E XIV Divn on 10th inst. & Lt BUCKELL Act/Adjt. on 11th inst. Lt. TEMPERLEY assumed command of 61st Co. RE from 10th inst.	
12th	No 1 Section relieve No 2 Section on CANAL Bank, No 2 go to new camp at A18d for work on ~~Divisional~~ Company Hutting	
	No 3 Section finish LANCASHIRE FARM Tramway and start on B Breastwork of C Line	
	No 4 Section Divisional Hutting at ELVERDINGHE.	

Instructions regarding War Diaries and Intelligence Summaries are contained in F. S. Regs., Part II. and the Staff Manual respectively. Title pages will be prepared in manuscript.

61st Field Co RE
14th Division

WAR DIARY
or
~~INTELLIGENCE SUMMARY~~

(Erase heading not required.)

January 1916

Army Form C. 2118.

Hour, Date, Place	Summary of Events and Information	Remarks and references to Appendices
13th	Work as on 12th, except No 4 Section worked in Camp on Trench Stores.	
14th	No 1 Section commenced work on GLIMPSE COTTAGE Tramway & continued work on CANAL BANK. No 2 Section at work on New Divisional Headquarters. No 3 Section on A & B Breastworks of C Line. No 4 Section go to new camp at A18d for Company Hutting.	
15th	As on 14th, Sapper JOHNSON, No 3 Section wounded.	
16th	Nos 1 ~~[struck out]~~ and 2 Sections as before; No 4 Section go to CANAL BANK for work. No 3 Section move to A18d for Company Hutting.	
17th–19th	No 1 section working on CANAL Bank, No 2 Section Divisional Hutting. No 3 Section Company Hutting at New Camp. No 4 Section at work on C Line and ~~[struck out]~~ BARD COTTAGE extension of Tramway. Sapper BALDERSTONE No 1 Section wounded on 17th. 2 Lt WILLMER went to hospital with nervous breakdown on 18th.	
20th	Major MACKESY resumes command of Company. No 1 Section Divisional Hutting. No 2 Section at work on CANAL Bank and relaying GLIMPSE COTTAGE Tramway. Nos 3 & 4 Sections as before	
21st–23rd	Work as on 20th. No 3 section relieve No 4 Section in evening of 23rd	
24–26	Nos 1 + 2 as on 20th. No 1 Section relieved No 2 in afternoon of 26th. No 3 Section working on Butts C11 & C12 & BARD COTTAGE Tramway; part of No 4 Coy Hutting at A18d, remainder on Trench Stores in Camp. Sapper NICOL wounded by bullet on 25th.	

1247 W 3299 200,000 (E) 8/14 J.B.C. & A. Forms/C. 2118/11.

61st Field Co. RE
14th Division

Instructions regarding War Diaries and Intelligence Summaries are contained in F. S. Regs., Part II. and the Staff Manual respectively. Title pages will be prepared in manuscript.

WAR DIARY
or
~~INTELLIGENCE SUMMARY~~
(Erase heading not required.)

January 1916

Army Form C. 2118.

Hour, Date, Place	Summary of Events and Information	Remarks and references to Appendices
27th – 30th	No 1 Section repairing Bridge 6A, constructing dugout for Dynamo, and relaying GLIMPSE COTTAGE Tramway. No 2 Section on Divisional Hutting. No 3 Section laying BARD COTTAGE Tramway, and working on C11 + C12 Breastworks. No 4 Section, on Company Hutting and Trench Stores; relieved No 3 section in afternoon of 30th. Sapper BRETTEL wounded on 30th	
31st	No 1 + 2 as on 30th. No 3 Section, trench stores + company hutting. No 4 section on BARD COTTAGE Tramway and C Line.	

[signature]
MAJOR R.E.
COMDG. 61ST FIELD Co. R. E

1247 W 3299 200,000 (E) 8/14 J.B.C. & A. Forms/C. 2118/11.

14

61st F.C.R.E.

Vol. 10

61st Field Co. RE

XW Divn

February 1916

Army Form C. 2118.

Instructions regarding War Diaries and Intelligence Summaries are contained in F. S. Regs., Part II. and the Staff Manual respectively. Title pages will be prepared in manuscript.

WAR DIARY
or
INTELLIGENCE SUMMARY.
(Erase heading not required.)

Place	Date	Hour	Summary of Events and Information	Remarks and references to Appendices
BRANDHOEK	1st–6th		No 1 Section on CANAL Bank repairing bridges and constructing dugouts; No 2 Section building Divisional Headquarters between ELVERDINGHE & POPERINGHE. No 3 Section sandbagging Signal Office at BRIELEN and Company Hutting at A18d. No 4 Section completed BARD COTTAGE Tramway and planking of GLIMPSE COTTAGE Tramway, continued wiring CANAL Line. Sapper MUNDAY wounded by shell on 3rd.	
"	7th–9th		No 1 Section at work on CANAL; returned to camp on 9th. No 2 Section working on ELVERDINGHE sector Divisional Hutting. No 3 Section at CANAL, packing up GLIMPSE COTTAGE Tramway and wiring CANAL Line. No 4 Section at work in Camp and on repairs at Divisional Headquarters	
"	10th		No's 1 & 4 Sections clearing wagons and packing up in Camp. No 2 Section returned to old camp from A18d. No 3 Section constructing dugouts at CANAL.	
"	11th		Company in Camp preparing to move	
"	12th		Company marched through STEENVOORDE to billets near OUDEZEELE France 16 miles	
OUDEZEELE	13–20		Company engaged in drill, pontooning etc. On the 17th the 41st Inf Bde including 61st Co RE was inspected by the C in C at WINNIZEELE	
"	21st		Company marched from OUDEZEELE at 10 am. for CASSELL station 6 miles and entrained.	
		4.40	Train left.	

T2134. Wt. W708–776. 500000. 4/15. Sir J. C. & S.

Instructions regarding War Diaries and Intelligence Summaries are contained in F. S. Regs., Part II. and the Staff Manual respectively. Title pages will be prepared in manuscript.

61st Field Co. RE
14th Division

WAR DIARY
or
INTELLIGENCE SUMMARY.
(Erase heading not required.)

February 1916

Army Form C. 2118.

Place	Date	Hour	Summary of Events and Information	Remarks and references to Appendices
	22nd	1.30am	Detrained at LONGUEAU. Marched through AMIENS to FLESSELLES. 9 miles	
FLESSELLES	23rd		Route March and tactical training.	
"	24th		Marched through BEAUVAL to PETIT OCCOCHES near DOULLENS 16 miles	
	25th		Marched through DOULLENS to SUS ST LEGER 12 miles. Snow blizzard; transport did not arrive till 11.30pm.	
SUS ST LEGER	26-27th		Rested at SUS ST LEGER.	
FOSSEUX	28th		Marched to FOSSEUX. 8 miles	
"	29th		Rested at FOSSEUX. Lts TEMPERLEY, FENWICK & BUCKELL to ARRAS to reconnoitre trenches.	

[signature] Major RE
OC 61 Fd Coy
4/3/16

T2134. Wt. W708-776. 500000. 4/15. Sir J. C. & S.

14

61 JERE

Vol

II

Officer i/c
A.G. Office
at the
Base

Herewith please receive
War Diary of 61st Field Co RE for
the month of March 1916

S.C.O.Tempey
Lt RE (SO)
OC 61 Co RE

4·4·16

61st Field Company
Royal Engineers
14th (Light) Division

March 1916.

WAR DIARY
or
~~INTELLIGENCE SUMMARY.~~
(Erase heading not required.)

Army Form C. 2118.

Instructions regarding War Diaries and Intelligence Summaries are contained in F. S. Regs., Part II. and the Staff Manual respectively. Title pages will be prepared in manuscript.

Place	Date	Hour	Summary of Events and Information	Remarks and references to Appendices
FOSSEUX	1st		Marched to DAINVILLE near ARRAS. 7 miles. Village entered after dark.	
DAINVILLE	2nd		Company arranging billets. Lts TEMPERLEY, FENWICK + BUCKELL to ARRAS to arrange billets and reconnoitre.	
do	3rd		Nos 2 + 4 Sections proceed to ARRAS, accomodated in CASERNE LEVIS under Lts FENWICK and BUCKELL	
ARRAS	4th		No 2 Section commenced digging new trench at St SAUVEUR and fixing fire steps in existing trenches	
			No 4 Section mining dugouts in CEMETERY east of ARRAS and making M.G. emplacement and dugouts in Railway Embankment east of ARRAS	
DAINVILLE			No 1 + 3 sections in DAINVILLE, mining dugouts, cleaning billets, erecting latrines etc.	
"	5th-12th		Work continued as on 4th	
ARRAS	13th		Nos 2 + 4 sections working east of ARRAS as before, joined by half No 1 Section in evening.	
DAINVILLE	"		No 1 Section in DAINVILLE mining dugouts, and camp duties	
BERNEVILLE	"		No 3 Section commenced work at BERNEVILLE; repairing baths, erecting latrines + ablution benches	
ARRAS	14th-31st		1/2 No 1 Section and No 2 Section working on the defences of St SAUVEUR	
"	"		No 4 Section working on defences of CEMETERY East of ARRAS and building Observation Post in BLANGY.	
BERNEVILLE SIMENCOURT	"		No 3 Section completed construction of Latrines in BERNEVILLE, repaired and improved the water supply and baths in BERNEVILLE + SIMENCOURT.	
DAINVILLE			1/2 No 1 Section worked on camp duties and provision of proper sanitary arrangements in DAINVILLE; commenced improvement of water supplies of WANQUETIN + WARLUS	

T2134. Wt. W708–776. 500000. 4/15. Sir J. C. & S.

Instructions regarding War Diaries and Intelligence Summaries are contained in F. S. Regs., Part II. and the Staff Manual respectively. Title pages will be prepared in manuscript.

WAR DIARY
or
INTELLIGENCE SUMMARY.
(Erase heading not required.)

Army Form C. 2118.

Place	Date	Hour	Summary of Events and Information	Remarks and references to Appendices
DAINVILLE	17 3/16		Lieut H.G. ROWLEY died of Cerebro spinal meningitis and was buried in ARRAS this night.	
			2/Lt. J.T. MORRIS went to Hospital as a contact case.	
	22 3/16		2/Lt. E.D. MOORE joined 61st Company and took charge of No 3 Section.	
	23 3/16		Major J.P. MACKESY, promoted Lt Colonel and appointed CRE 31st Division, while on leave in England. Lt E.E.V. TEMPERLEY R.E.(SR) assumed command of 61st Field Co R.E.	
	29 3/16		2/Lt J.T. MORRIS returned from Hospital. 1 Section of 2/1st London Fd. Co R.E. attached for instruction and work on defences East of ARRAS	

E.E.V. Temperley Lieut R.E. (SR)
for O.C. 61st FIELD Co. R.E.

T2134. Wt. W708–776. 500000. 4/15. Sir J. C. & S.

61st Field Co. R.E. 14th Division

61 F Co RE

Vol 12

Instructions regarding War Diaries and Intelligence Summaries are contained in F. S. Regs., Part II. and the Staff Manual respectively. Title pages will be prepared in manuscript.

WAR DIARY or ~~INTELLIGENCE SUMMARY~~.

(*Erase heading not required.*)

XIV

April 1916

Army Form C. 2118.

Place	Date	Hour	Summary of Events and Information	Remarks and references to Appendices
			FRONT LINE WORK:–	
ARRAS.	1st to 30th –		No 4 Section:–	
BLANGY			(i). O.P. for artillery comfection. The site of this was in the CHATEAU ROUGE in BLANGY and from the Post an excellent view was obtained of the German lines – The Post was some 200 yds behind our ~~[illegible]~~ lines but owing to ~~[illegible]~~ its site in amongst the debris of a house in absolute ruins excellent concealment was obtained – The double tube of steel with which the Post was made was handed over to us by the French as these articles do not seem to be supplied by the British. See APPENDIX	No I
CEMETERY			(ii). Four mined dugouts, three of which are completed except for the emergency exit – Each dugout is 30' x 7' inside dimension and 6' high – With double bunks erected this gives accomodation for 20 men – ~~14 20~~ ~~[illegible]~~ Each dugout has 14' of cover of undisturbed earth –	
"			(ii). S.A.A. Store. This was made on the cut & fill principle and cover to this was given as in sketch. See APPENDIX No II	
"			(iii). Off: Dugout. Size 7' x 12' Unfinished –	

T2134. Wt. W708–776. 500000. 4/15. Sir J. C. & S.

61st Field Coy R.E.
14th Division

Sheet II

WAR DIARY
or
~~INTELLIGENCE SUMMARY~~.
(Erase heading not required.)

April 1916

Army Form C. 2118.

Instructions regarding War Diaries and Intelligence Summaries are contained in F. S. Regs., Part II. and the Staff Manual respectively. Title pages will be prepared in manuscript.

Place	Date	Hour	Summary of Events and Information	Remarks and references to Appendices
Ry. BANK N. of CEMETERY			(iv). Bomb Store completed – } These dugouts were mined into the (v). Three Dugouts for Bombers completed } Ry. Embankment – (vi) One old dugout for Bn Bombing Officer ~~completed~~ renovated – (vii). BDE. Battle Hqs. – An old cellar was found and was strengthened as shown in detail in APPENDIX No III – An emergency exit is in course of construction at the end of the cellar. About 10' of cover in addition to the debris of the house ~~will~~ will exist – Work not finished	III
ST SAVEUR			(viii). An O.P. for artillery in course of construction – Work not finished – Detailed Description in APPENDIX No ~~III~~ IV (ix). In addition to the above ~~was~~ a number of petty works were carried out e.g. clearing trenches of CEMETERY Defences, blowing up unexploded trench mortars and shells, arrangements for the blocking of communication trenches –	IV

61st Field Coy R.E.
14th Divn.

Sheet III

Instructions regarding War Diaries and Intelligence Summaries are contained in F. S. Regs., Part II. and the Staff Manual respectively. Title pages will be prepared in manuscript.

WAR DIARY
or
INTELLIGENCE SUMMARY.
(*Erase heading not required.*)

April 1916

Army Form C. 2118.

Place	Date	Hour	Summary of Events and Information	Remarks and references to Appendices
ARRAS	1st–17th		No 2 Section :-	
			(i). 700 yards of the "B" line S. of St SAVEUR reclaimed, fire step built, parapet revetted in each fire bay. The revetting in this case was done by expanded metal and angle iron pickets which proved very satisfactory. Wire strengthened in front.	
			(ii) S.A.A. Store completed.	
			(iii). Mined dugout for machine gunners completed.	
			(iv). New trenches dug and old trenches of the inner St SAVEUR Defences ~~are~~ repaired.	
			(v). ~~[illegible]~~ Machine gun emplacement commenced by the French, continued. Ferro-concrete roof and sides put in.	
			(vi). Three French cut & fill dugouts ~~[illegible]~~ strengthened and finished.	
"	1–6th		½ of No 1 Sec. worked with No 2 Sec.	
"	1–11th		1 Section of 2/1st LONDON FD. Coy R.E. attached for instruction and worked with Nos 2 & 4 Sections as required.	
	12th–30th		1 Section of 2/2nd LONDON FD. Coy R.E. ~~[illegible]~~ took the place of the 2/1st.	

T2134. Wt. W708–776. 500000. 4/15. Sir J. C. & S.

61st Field Co RE
14th Div.

Sheet IV

WAR DIARY
or
INTELLIGENCE SUMMARY.
(Erase heading not required.)

Army Form C. 2118.

Instructions regarding War Diaries and Intelligence Summaries are contained in F. S. Regs., Part II. and the Staff Manual respectively. Title pages will be prepared in manuscript.

April 1916

Place	Date	Hour	Summary of Events and Information	Remarks and references to Appendices
ARRAS	18th - 30th.		No 3 Section:-	
			This took over the whole work of No 2 Section, which was unfinished, and commenced no new work beyond doing some wiring round the Inner Defences of ST SAVEUR.	
			The Sections when back at DAINVILLE worked on	
			(i) Baths and water supply at SIMENCOURT.	
			(ii). Erected latrines, improved baths, at BERNEVILLE	
			(iii). Build baths & pack store for 42nd Fd Amb at WANQUETIN.	
			Also mended pumps and did water supply at same place.	
			(iv). Built latrines, ablution benches, mended wells, and commenced bunking at WARLUS.	
			(v). Camp work & commenced bunking barns in DAINVILLE.	
DAINVILLE			Lt Col J.P. MACKESY left for 31st Division on 4th. Capt M.E. MORGAN R.E. assumed command of 61st Coy R.E. on 15th and returned to 62nd C.R.E. on 25th after handing over to Captain E.F.W. LEES R.E. 2/Lt J.T. MORRIS went to England on 26th.	

E.F.W. Lees
Capt RE
O.C. 61st Fd Coy RE

T2134. Wt. W708—776. 500000. 4/15. Sir J. C. & S.

61st Field Co RE
14th Div.
WAR DIARY. April 1916

APPENDIX No I

Report on O.P. erected in CHATEAU ROUGE

The O.P. consists of a double tube of steel $\frac{1}{8}$" thick with 4" concrete between the two skins of steel & covered with a cupola of the same material. It is 10'0" high & mounted on a brick pedestal 5'½ high.

The arch of the cellar was cut thro' & the debris from above removed until what was the roof of the chateau was reached. This was left to cover the hole & also to conceal the O.P. when in position.

The brick pedestal was built to the required height & the steel tube [illegible] mounted in position & filled with concrete, & the bricks continued up to the roof outside the steel to [illegible] support the arch which had been cut thro'. Above the roof the tube was surrounded by 18" of rough concrete reinforced with vertical angle iron bars to prevent shearing the top was covered with 9" concrete in which bars of pig iron were imbedded to form a shell burster the whole being covered over with about 2 ft of debris of brick & timber. Finally the debris was cleared away from in front of the loophole & disguised by pieces of timber. There is about 10 to 12 ft of earth in front of the actual loophole in the steel

Appendix I Sheet II

The labour employed was 1 N.C.O & 2 sprs constructing the O.P. 1 N.C.O. with 10 gunners to carry up materials.
No. of man hours taken in construction alone is 350. This does not include time & labour spent in getting up materials which would account for another 300 m.h.

Material used 23 bags cement
150 sandbags sand & gravel.
5000 bricks (approx)
400 galls water (")
10 bars pig iron
1 ladder
4 sections, 1 top 1 door steel shelter

The whole of the work was carried out from below by day with the exception of putting the cement & pig iron on the top & clearing the debris from in front of loophole which had to be done by night.

2.4.16.

C.D. ? Lt R.E.

Appendix I Sheet III

Sectional Elevation of O.P.

Debris of house

Bars of [illegible] iron set in concrete

Loophole 150° arc

1st floor of house

Cellar

ladder

floor of cellar

Section thro' A A

Scale 1 sq to 1 ft

step

4in concrete

steel door

APPENDIX No II

61st Field Co RE
14th Div
War Diary. April
1916

S.A.A. STORE –

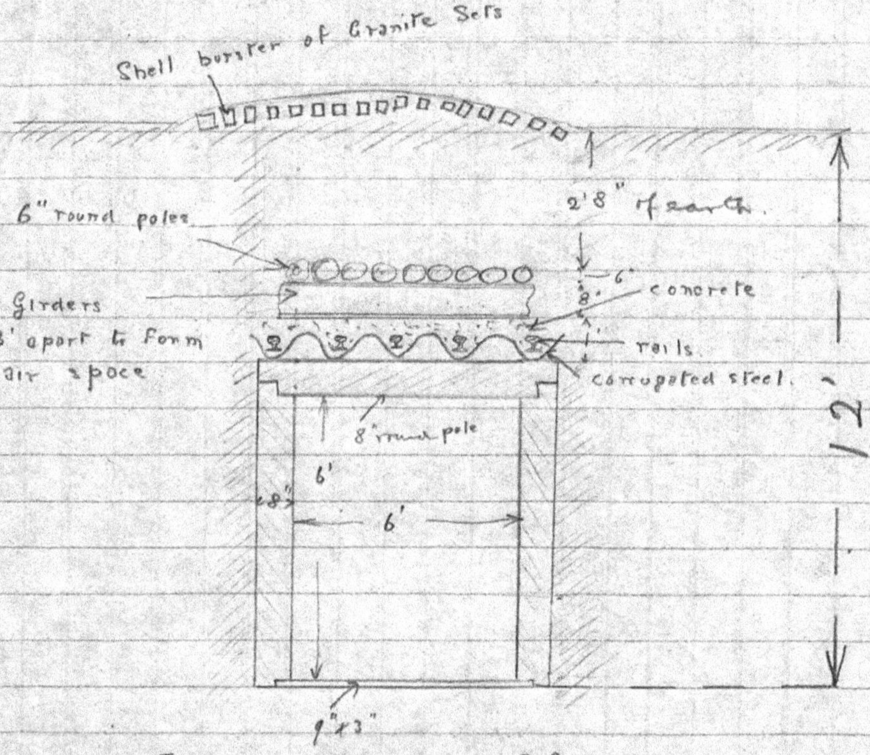

Shell burster of Granite Sets

2'8" of earth.

6" round poles

6"

Girders
3' apart to form
air space

8"

concrete

rails

corrugated steel.

8" round pole

12'

6'

8"

6'

9"x3"

Frames spaced 3 ft apart.

SIZE OF STORE – 6 FT. CUBE.

APPENDIX No. III

Report on Concrete Arch strengthening to cellar.

The cellar ~~[illegible]~~ is 20 ft long by 8' 6" wide at the floor & ab[illegible] 7 ft high with an curved roof. It is dug out of the natural earth with no support to it.

The foundation to the arch consists of a framework of $2\frac{1}{2}" \times 2"$ I section steel bent in a semicircle & braced together at 3'6" intervals with $1" \times \frac{1}{4}"$ flat iron. The earth was cut away round the framework to a depth of 9" to 1 ft & the space filled with concrete, the inner 3" being fine concrete & the rest coarse. Reinforcement of the arch was provided by horizontal lengths of $1\frac{1}{2}"$ L iron at intervals of 6" top of the arch & by $1\frac{1}{4}"$ channel iron bent to the curve of the arch & spaced at 3" intervals on the lower side of the arch.

C. D. [illegible]
[illegible]

2. 5. 16

61st Field Coy RE
14th Division
War Diary April 1916

Vertical Section of Arch Lining Cave

Natural Earth

9" concrete ring

$2\frac{1}{2}" \times 2"$ R.S. I section steel spaced 2'6" centres

$1" \times \frac{1}{4}"$ iron distance pieces

$1\frac{1}{2}"$ L iron 6" centres running longitudinally

6'0"

7'0"

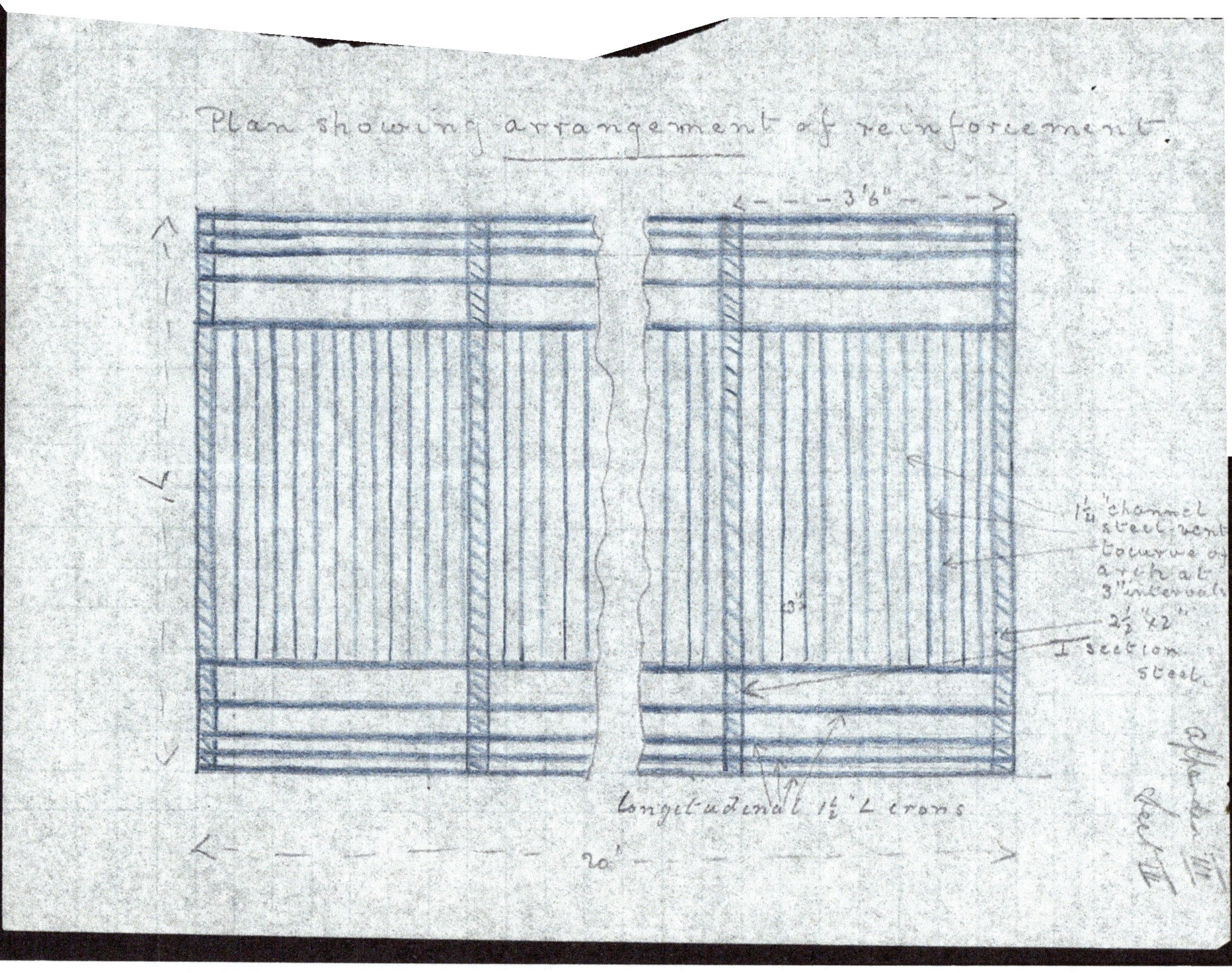

Plan showing arrangement of reinforcement.
3'6"
7'
3"
1¼" channel steel vent to curve of arch at 3" intervals
2½" x 2" I section steel.
longitudinal 1½" L irons
20'
Chapter VII
Sect. II

APPENDIX No. ~~III~~ IV

Report on O.P. in S.T. SAUVEUR

6th Field Co RE
14 Divn
WAR
DIARY
April 1916

The O.P. is built in a small chalk house 14' square & about 36' high. The first floor is about 11 to 12 ft from ground level & is supported by a brick arch.

The O.P. consists of two lattice work girders made of 2¾" L iron with 1½" L iron braces. They are 2' sq at the top, 13'6" high & braced together. The platform is 7'×5' overall made of 3/16" wrought steel plate carried on 4 transoms of 2½" L iron. This carries a box of ⅛" steel plate 4' high at the sides & 6'6" high at the ridge point & this is lined with 6" concrete.

The roof consists of a continuous layer of L iron with one side parallel to the slope of the roof the other at right angles, the spaces in between being filled with concrete. Ten of these L irons are bolted to the sides to give lateral strength the remainder are supported by the concrete wall. Access is obtained thro a hole in the floor.

The stanchions are strutted behind & the arch supported by a brick & concrete pillar 3'6" by 8' immediately below the weight, a hole being cut thro the crown for access to the O.P.

2.5.16

[illegible] Lt RE.

Sectional Elevation of O.P. (side view)

Appendix IX
Sheet II

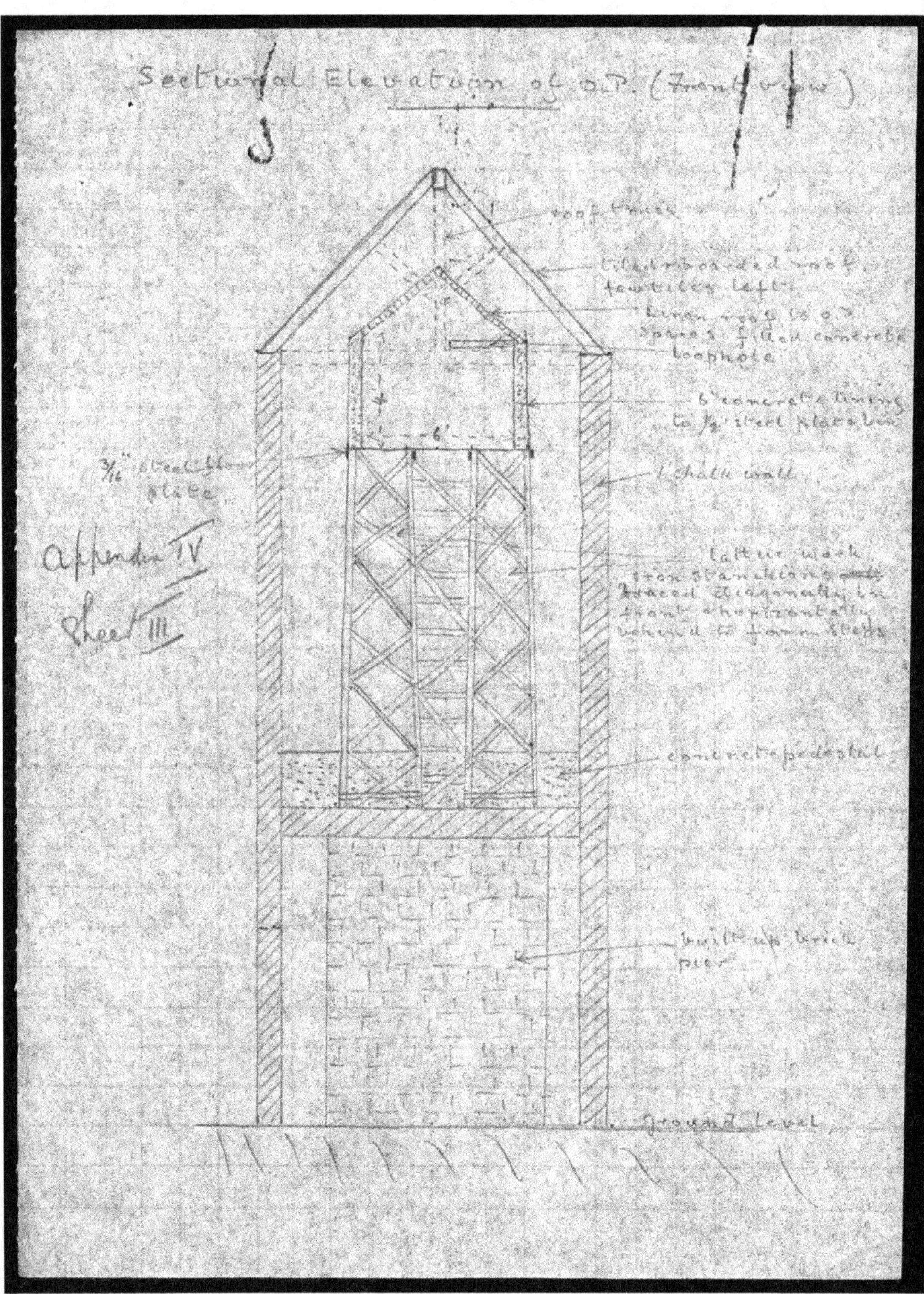
Sectional Elevation of O.P. (Front view)
roof truss
tiled boarded roof, few tiles left
Linen roof to O.P.
spaces filled concrete
loophole
6' concrete lining
3/16" steel floor plate
chalk wall
lattice work iron stanchions braced diagonally in front & horizontally behind to form steps
concrete pedestal
built up brick pier
Ground level
Appendix IV
Sheet III

61st FIELD COY. R.E. 14th DIVISION

Sheet 1 — 61 F.C.R.E. — Army Form C. 2118. — Vol 13 — XIV

Instructions regarding War Diaries and Intelligence Summaries are contained in F. S. Regs., Part II. and the Staff Manual respectively. Title pages will be prepared in manuscript.

WAR DIARY
or
~~INTELLIGENCE SUMMARY.~~
(Erase heading not required.)

May 1916

Place	Date	Hour	Summary of Events and Information	Remarks and references to Appendices
ARRAS			FRONT LINE WORK:–	
			No. 4 Sect	
	1st–4th.		Work on items below continued and handed over to the 1/2nd HOME COUNTIES of the 5th Divn.	
			(i). Dugout in Ry. Embankment, which was completed except for finishing off the bunks for 10 men.–	
			(ii) 4 mined dugouts for CEMETERY Garrison. In 3 the excavation was completed and the fitting of bunks for 20 men was commenced and in the 4th dugout the entrance was complete and 10 feet of excavation were completed.–	
			(iii). Dugout for 2 officers of CEMETERY Garrison.–	
			(iv). Bde. Battle Hqs. ~~[illegible]~~ The reinforced concrete arch in one cellar completed and both entrances require finishing.–	
			(v). O.P. in ST SAVEUR completed except for finishing off the roof and a concrete pedestal.–	
			(vi). Repairs to Southern fire trenches in CEMETERY Defences.–	

T2134. Wt. W708–776. 500000. 4/15. Sir J. C. & S.

61st FIELD COY. R.E.
14th DIVISION

Sheet II

Instructions regarding War Diaries and Intelligence Summaries are contained in F. S. Regs., Part II. and the Staff Manual respectively. Title pages will be prepared in manuscript.

WAR DIARY
or
~~INTELLIGENCE SUMMARY~~.
(Erase heading not required.)

May

Army Form C. 2118.

Place	Date	Hour	Summary of Events and Information	Remarks and references to Appendices
			No 3 Sect.	
ARRAS.	1st–4th.		Work on items below continued and handed over to 1/2nd HOME COUNTIES FD. Coy RE. of the 5th Div.	
			(i). Wiring up to CAMBRAI ROAD on NORTH side of ST SAVEUR INNER Defences finished with wire 3 to 4 bays thick.	
			(ii). Fire trench NORTH of ST SAVEUR DEFENCES of ST SAVEUR completed.	
			(iii). Fire trenches, SOUTH of CAMBRAI ROAD improved.	
			(iv). Dugout for M.G. emplacement on CAMBRAI ROAD in the ST SAVEUR DEFENCES commenced.	
			MAP of SECTOR attached & marked I. Map of ST SAVEUR attached & marked II.	
			BACK WORK:-	
			No 1 Sect.	
WANQUENTIN	1st–22nd.		Worked on fitting up huts in barns, water supply, baths etc for 42nd FD. AMB.	
	22nd		Commenced training.	

T2134. Wt. W708–776. 500000. 4/15. Sir J. C. & S.

61st Field Co R.E. 14th Division

War Diary April 1916

Appendix I. Map of Sector.

33e Division

5000e

Quartier de Blangy

Tirage du 14 Novembre 1915

61st FIELD COY. R.E. — 14th DIVISION

Sheet III

Army Form C. 2118.

WAR DIARY
or
~~INTELLIGENCE SUMMARY.~~
(Erase heading not required.)

Instructions regarding War Diaries and Intelligence Summaries are contained in F. S. Regs., Part II. and the Staff Manual respectively. Title pages will be prepared in manuscript.

May 1916

Place	Date	Hour	Summary of Events and Information	Remarks and references to Appendices
			No 2 Sect.	
	2nd		moved from DAINVILLE to WANQUENTIN	
WANQUENTIN	2nd–23rd		Worked on bunks in barns, water supply, fitting up horse troughs etc.	
	24th		Commenced training –	
			No 3 Sect.	
	4th		Returned from ARRAS to DAINVILLE.	
	5th–17th		Worked in DAINVILLE on bunking barns, repairing pumps etc –	
	17th		moved to WANQUENTIN.	
	22nd		Commenced training –	
			No 4 Sect.	
	4th		Returned from ARRAS to DAINVILLE	
	5th–23rd		Worked at WARLUS on water supply, fitting up horse troughs and bunking – On the 17th to 23rd it lived in billets in WARLUS –	
	24th		Commenced training –	

1577 Wt. W10791/1773 500,000 1/15 D. D. & L. A.D.S.S./Forms/C. 2118.

Sheet IV

61st Field Coy R.E. /14th Division.

Instructions regarding War Diaries and Intelligence Summaries are contained in F. S. Regs., Part II. and the Staff Manual respectively. Title pages will be prepared in manuscript.

WAR DIARY
or
~~INTELLIGENCE SUMMARY.~~
(Erase heading not required.)

May 1916

Army Form C. 2118.

Place	Date	Hour	Summary of Events and Information	Remarks and references to Appendices
			Company training:-	
WANQUETIN	22-31		This training was intended to last a fortnight and included, drill, musketry practice, gas lectures and drill, bombing, Weldon trestle and ordinary trestle bridging, use of explosives, day and night wiring, consolidation of positions.	
DAINVILLE	1		2Lt. E.R. FOSTER joined Company and took command of No1 Section	

1577 Wt. W10791/1773 500,000 1/15 D. D. & L. A.D.S.S./Forms/C. 2118.

Officer i/c
A G's Office
at the Base

Herewith please receive
War Diary of 61st Field Coy R.E.
14th Division, for the month of
June 1916

E. C. Ottenway [illegible]

61st FIELD COMPANY
Date 3/7/16
ROYAL ENGINEERS

[illegible]
for
O.C. 61st Fd. C. R.E.

Sheet I XIV June

Army Form C. 2118.

VOL 14

Instructions regarding War Diaries and Intelligence Summaries are contained in F. S. Regs., Part II. and the Staff Manual respectively. Title pages will be prepared in manuscript.

WAR DIARY
or
~~INTELLIGENCE SUMMARY~~
(Erase heading not required.)

61st Field Company RE

	Hour, Date, Place	Summary of Events and Information	Remarks and references to Appendices
June 1st – 5th	WANQUETIN	Company training. The programme outlined in last month's War Diary was successfully completed: the Corps Commander inspected the Company on the afternoon of the 3rd: during this period, certain men were employed on water supply and the construction of baths in the village.	
6th	WANQUETIN	HQ and No 2 Section	
	To DAINVILLE	Nos 1, 3 and 4 Sections.	
7th	To ARRAS	No 3 Section	
	To AGNY	Nos 1 and 4 Sections	
	To DAINVILLE	HQ and No 2 Section.	
8th – 17th	ARRAS	No 3 Section working on ARRAS defences under the direction of the Corps.	
	AGNY	Nos 1 and 3 Sections employed in G Sector: chiefly on the following: CRINCHON Strong point. / Mined dug-outs in I.S. line near GUN and GRAVEL streets commenced. Protected O.P.s. AGNY Dressing Station. Left Sector Dressing Station. Water supply AGNY – erection of tanks.	
	DAINVILLE	No 2 Section employed on bunking, etc: erection of 2 huts for officers commenced	
night of 17th	To ARRAS.	No 4 Section.	
	To AGNY	No 2 Section.	
	To DAINVILLE	No 3 Section	
18th + 19th	ARRAS	No 4 Section working on ARRAS defences under Corps Orders	
	AGNY	Nos 1 and 2 Sections employed on the various works shown above.	
	DAINVILLE.	No 3 Section on bunking and officers' huts.	

1247 W 3299 200,000 (E) 8/14 J.B.C. & A. Forms/C. 2118/11.

Instructions regarding War Diaries and Intelligence Summaries are contained in F. S. Regs., Part II. and the Staff Manual respectively. Title pages will be prepared in manuscript.

WAR DIARY
or
~~INTELLIGENCE SUMMARY~~
(Erase heading not required.)

Sheet II

Army Form C. 2118.

61st Field Coy RE

Hour, Date, Place		Summary of Events and Information	Remarks and references to Appendices
Evening of 19th	To ARRAS	Nos 1, 2, and 3 sections, after having been received to take over I Sector (Left) from 1/2 Home Co RE, and J sector from 59th Field Coy RE.	
20th	ARRAS	Taking over the work from the outgoing Coys: No 4 section rejoined company for work.	
21st to 30th	ARRAS	No 3 section employed as follows:– Shelter underneath Rlway Bridge N.W. of Cemetery: handed over to Kings Liverpool Regt on 25th. Officers' Shelter in CEMETERY: handed over to King's Liverpool Regiment on 25th. Shelter for T.M.B Detachment IRON STREET: completed 24th. Shelter for " " " INCOME TAX: in hand on 30th. Grenade Store, Rlway Embankment: in hand on 30th O.P. (R.A.) ST SAUVEUR: work continued on 24th: in hand on 30th. Shelter ST SAUVEUR: work continued on 26th: in hand on 30th M.G. emplacement in IVORY Street: commenced 29th: " " " INNS OF COURT: commenced 29th. Cut and cover dug-out INNS OF COURT: continued 29th. No 2 section employed as follows:– Shelter for T.M.B: FEBRUARY AVENUE: work suspended on 25th Consolidating craters: wiring of right and left craters completed by 30th: fair progress made by infantry working parties (80 per night) Curved Iron shelters: CANDLE FACTORY: work made excellent progress, 40 infantry in two reliefs being employed: one shelter fixed and covered, one fixed, and excavation for 3rd nearly completed on 30th.	no work has since been done on the

Sheet II

Army Form C. 2118.

Instructions regarding War Diaries and Intelligence Summaries are contained in F. S. Regs., Part II. and the Staff Manual respectively. Title pages will be prepared in manuscript.

WAR DIARY

~~or~~

~~INTELLIGENCE SUMMARY~~

(Erase heading not required.)

61st Field Coy R.E.

June	Hour, Date, Place	Summary of Events and Information	Remarks and references to Appendices
21st – 30th	ARRAS	No 4 section employed as follows:-	
		Mined shelter for M.G. Det. AUGUST AVENUE: work suspended on 29th	
		Mined First Aid Post off AUGUST AVENUE: work in hand on 30th – good progress and generally an excellent piece of work.	
		Trench shelter J 86 – work commenced on 29th	
		Trench shelter J 84, repairs to – work commenced on 29th	
		No 1 section employed as follows:-	
		Water Supply to Redoubt Line: work taken over from 59th Coy well advanced: engine room complete: water to CANDLE FACTORY and Battn Hqs. J.2 sector by 30th.	
		Progress on all works somewhat hampered by bad weather.	
		The mounted section did not move to DAINVILLE, on leaving WANQUETIN, but were accommodated at WATELUS.	
		Mounted section won the inter section shooting competition held during training. Both horses and vehicles well turned out.	
		E.W. Lees Major R.E. O.C. 61st Coy RE	

1247 W 3299 200,000 (E) 8/14 J.B.C. & A. Forms/C. 2118/11.

Instructions regarding War Diaries and Intelligence Summaries are contained in F. S. Regs., Part II. and the Staff Manual respectively. Title pages will be prepared in manuscript.

WAR DIARY

~~or~~

~~INTELLIGENCE SUMMARY~~

(Erase heading not required.)

Army Form C. 2118.

34 Feeny

VOL 15

JULY 1916

61st Field Coy R.E.

Hour, Date, Place	Summary of Events and Information	Remarks and references to Appendices
July 1st to 27th	At ARRAS: the main features of the work undertaken in this time are given in Appendix I.	
July 28th	Coy from ARRAS to BRIQUETERIE between WARLUS and WANQUETIN	weather very hot: Coy stood marches well.
July 29th	" " BRIQUETERIE to SUS-ST-LEGER	
July 30th	" " SUS-ST-LEGER to BONNIERES.	
July 31st	Company at BONNIERES: parade in drill order 9 a.m. Gas helmet drill 10 a.m onwards.	

Appendix I.

Water Supply. Water was laid on to FORESTIER, NICOLLS, and BOSKT Redoubts, and to Batt.n Hqs and Cookhouses in J.1 and J.2, and the work completed on 15.7.16. The system was a success.

Trench Tramway. A trench tramway, running along OCTOBER AVENUE, from CANDLE WORKS to SUPPORT Line (1500x) was commenced on 14.7.16 – by 28.7.16 the track was laid for a distance of 1000x, and Excavation had reached 1200x. A working party of 300 Infantry was employed, chiefly by night, and an extra section of RE was attached to the Company, first from the 67th Coy RE, and then from 1/4 A.T. Coy RE: the work was considerably hindered by constant changes in the personnel of the working parties.

Machine Gun Emplacements. Two completed and three commenced.

1247 W 3299 200,000 (E) 8/14 J.B.C. & A. Forms/C. 2118/11.

Instructions regarding War Diaries and Intelligence Summaries are contained in F. S. Regs., Part II. and the Staff Manual respectively. Title pages will be prepared in manuscript.

WAR DIARY
~~or~~
~~INTELLIGENCE SUMMARY~~

(Erase heading not required.)

Army Form C. 2118.

July 1916 Sheet I

61st Coy R.E.

Hour, Date, Place	Summary of Events and Information	Remarks and references to Appendices
	Shell proof shelters	
	6 mined shelters completed.	
	1 Cut and cover shelter completed	
	1 mined Dressing station ~~with room~~ for M.O completed.	
	Trench shelters	
	5 erected.	
	Miscellaneous	
	Much work was done on the three craters in J.2 sector – The left ~~right~~ and centre craters were handed over to the Pioneers in the middle of the month – the right crater had been practically completed by the time the company left.	
	The Petit chateau near the BAUDIMONT entrance to ARRAS was demolished.	
	One Section of the company was lent for work on the K. Craters from the 7th to the 17th.	
	[signature] Major RE O.C. 61st Coy RE	

1247 W 3299 200,000 (E) 8/14 J.B.C. & A. Forms/C. 2118/11.

14th Division

61st FIELD COMPANY

ROYAL ENGINEERS

A U G U S T   1 9 1 6

Attached: Report on Operations.

C.R.E.

Herewith report on yesterday's operations, as affecting this company.

2. The task of the Company was to construct and wire 3 strong points, each for a platoon at

(a) Enemy Salient at S.18.d.6.5. (MARS)

(b) Point where ALE ALLEY enters DELVILLE WOOD (VENUS).

(c) Junction of German trenches at S.18.b.7 (SATURN)

3. The necessary stores for each strong point were collected in dumps at S.18.c.7.9, S.18.a.5. and S.18.a.5.4, on the night of the 16th: the dumps were inspected on the evening of the 17th by an officer, and arrangements made to make up certain deficiencies.

4. The sections paraded at 6.45 a.m. on the 18th instant, picked up their respective platoons of pioneers at POMMIER Redoubt and proceeded to their assembly places as follows.

Section	Assembly Trench	Work
No. 4.	ANGLE Trench	MARS.
No. 1	— ditto —	VENUS
No. 2.	C.T. S.18.a.9½.9 to S.18.a central.	SATURN.
No. 3	Corps line, right resting on CROCIFIX ALLEY.	In reserve.

5. The Brigade instructions were as follows:—
"The Section Officers R.E. will be responsible for keeping themselves informed of what is happening, and seizing the opportunity of advancing and getting to work. They should not move, however, until the consolidation of the line is well begun".
All the Section Officers showed great determination in pushing forward to find out what was going on: it was while doing this that Lieut BUCKLE was wounded.

6. It was never possible at any time to get any work done on VENUS and SATURN: the enemy being in possession of these points throughout the battle, except for a short period after the assault when I believe the site for VENUS was in our hands, but we were bombed out.
Two sections R.E. and two platoons Pioneers did not therefore succeed in their tasks — they were in cramped trenches close behind the front line from 10 a.m. on the 18th to 4 a.m. on the 19th, at times under heavy shell fire.

7. MARS was dug (a rough sketch is attached) and surrounded with a row of French Wire interlaced with barbed wire.
Time, and the fact that they were crowded with men, prevented us straightening the entering trenches at A and B.

The taping out of the new trench was taken in hand at 3.45 p.m., and, except when interrupted by heavy shelling, work continued until 9 p.m. Sappers and pioneers were hopelessly mixed up with the assaulting infantry, and the greatest difficulty was experienced in getting up stores through the barrage behind the captured line. The first carrying party never reached the strong point at all. The second party, formed by putting sappers onto the digging in the strong point instead of pioneers, started 13 strong, and arrived 5 strong. It then became necessary to use some sappers for carrying, the progress of the work slowing down considerably. Eventually, however, the work shown in the sketch was completed.

8. The casualties were very slight – only 10% of the ~~men~~ R.E. employed: the section officers showed great judgement in moving their men about to avoid heavy shelling.

9. Generally, from the R.E. ~~of~~ point of view, it was a thoroughly unsatisfactory day, only one point out of the three being constructed – the enemy being in possession of the other two sites. The following points came prominently to notice

(a). The infantry working parties *must* be attached for at least a week beforehand living with the R.E. company and getting to know them.

(b). R.E. and working parties should ~~have~~ not be held in any position where they can get mixed up with assaulting troops: the CORPS line would have been far and away the most suitable place in this case.

(c). A strong point should not be in a line of trenches just captured by infantry – if it is absolutely necessary that it should be, then arrangements must be made for the victorious infantry to evacuate the portion of trench to be converted.

(d). Two ~~section~~ runners per section are necessary.

19/8/16

[illegible]
Major R.E.
O.C. 61st Div. R.E.

Instructions regarding War Diaries and Intelligence Summaries are contained in F. S. Regs., Part II. and the Staff Manual respectively. Title pages will be prepared in manuscript.

WAR DIARY

~~or~~

~~INTELLIGENCE SUMMARY.~~

(*Erase heading not required.*)

Army Form C. 2118.

61st Field Coy. RE.

Place	Date	Hour	Summary of Events and Information	Remarks and references to Appendices
BONNIERES	1st	–	Marched to GRIMONT.	
GRIMONT.	2nd	–	Physical Drill: rapid wiring	
" "	3rd	–	Physical Drill: ½ Coy route march and baths: ½ Coy rapid wiring	
" "	4th	–	——— ditto ———	
" "	5th	–	Route march 14 miles: night: laying out 2 platoon strong points and wiring same.	
" "	6th	–	Transport to COISY: company day off.	
" "	7th	–	To CANDAS: by tactical train to MERICOURT: by march to camp between DERNANCOURT ~~[illegible]~~ and ALBERT.	
Camp	8th–11th	–	Drill: rapid wiring: gas helmet drill each day.	
" "	12th	–	To bivouac near MAMETZ: (F.4.d.1.2)	
MAMETZ	13th	–	Clearing CRUCIFIX ALLEY: cutting under railway: burying two bodies.	
" "	14th	–	CRUCIFIX ALLEY completed to YORK TRENCH: 450 yards wire apron put up in front of YORK TRENCH: LEES SUPPORT laid out: to SAVOY trench, to reconnoitre work.	
" "	15th	–	SAVOY Trench taken in hand: 2 sections RE. 1 Coy Pioneers: 11½ fire bays ~~but~~ commenced: good progress: 1 hours work to complete. LEES SUPPORT: 2 sections RE 300 infantry: fair progress – work difficult owing to trees, roots, crump holes, etc.	
" "	16th	–	SAVOY Trench: work on fire bays continued: 7 sites for open M.G. Emplacements, with deep trench for gun team, selected and laid out. O.C. reconnaissance for continuation of SAVOY trench in front of LONGUEVAL. LEES SUPPORT: digging continued: trench to 4' except in 3 or 4 places: 350x of wire opposite central part of trench erected.	

T2134. Wt. W708–776. 500000. 4/15. Sir J. C. & S.

Army Form C. 2118.

Instructions regarding War Diaries and Intelligence Summaries are contained in F. S. Regs., Part II. and the Staff Manual respectively. Title pages will be prepared in manuscript.

WAR DIARY ~~or~~ ~~INTELLIGENCE SUMMARY~~.

(*Erase heading not required.*)

61st Field Coy RE.

Place	Date	Hour	Summary of Events and Information	Remarks and references to Appendices
MAMETZ	17th	–	Resting.	
" "	18th	–	Operation: copy of my original report attached: Lieut BUCKLE wounded.	
" "	19th	–	Company returned to their bivouacs about 6 a.m., and did no work beyond a parade in the afternoon for detailed inspection of Kits, equipment, etc, etc.	
" "	20th	–	My copies of the Progress Reports undecipherable on account of rain.	
" "	21st	–	(as above)	
" "	22nd	–	C.T. from S.18 a.01 to S.17.b.82. C.T. from S.17.b.84 to Support Line about S.17.b.97 } No working party available: Sappers made fair progress.	
			Work continued on Splinterproofs in Old German Trench N. of ~~billet~~ bivouac.	
" "	23rd	–	Excavating for splinterproof shelter 36'x6'x6' at S.23.c.6.2 Excavation completed.	
			" " 2 splinterproof shelters each 10'x10'x6' at S.18c 5.6 " " " (top of LONGUEVAL ALLEY).	
			Improving approaches to gallery S.17.b.83 (LONGUEVAL village).	
" "			Making frames for Sailcloths. 2nd Lieut CLOUSTON joined Company.	
" "	24th	–	Making and carrying frames for 3 splinterproof shelters.	
			Making shelter for 3 stretcher cases in LONGUEVAL ALLEY. completed.	
			Making frames for Sailcloths.	

T2134. Wt. W708—776. 500000. 4/15. Sir J. C. & S.

Army Form C. 2118.

Instructions regarding War Diaries and Intelligence Summaries are contained in F. S. Regs., Part II. and the Staff Manual respectively. Title pages will be prepared in manuscript.

~~INTELLIGENCE SUMMARY~~.

(Erase heading not required.)

61st Field Coy RE.

Place	Date	Hour	Summary of Events and Information	Remarks and references to Appendices
MAMETZ	25th	–	Splinterproof shelters at S.23.c.6.2 and S.18.c.5.6 completed.	
			Approaches to gallery S.17.b.8.3 completed: taken over as a Battn. HQ.	
" "	26th	–	Splinterproof shelter at S.23a 6½.7 (36'×6'×6') commenced.	
			" " " " S.18.c.4.6 (12'×6'×6') commenced.	
			Frames for splinterproofs and sailcloths.	
" "	27th	–	Excavation for splinterproof shelters at S.23.a.6½.7 and S.18.c.4.6. completed.	
			Shelter for 3 stretcher cases made near S.18.c.4.6.	
			Frames for splinterproofs and sailcloths.	
" "	28th	–	Splinterproof shelters at S.23.a.6½.7 and S.18.c.4.6 completed.	
			Small shelter near Battn. HQ. (Rear of LONGUEVAL ALLEY) re-roofed: completed.	
			Frames for splinterproofs & sailcloths.	
			C.T. from CRUCIFIX ALLEY to ANGLE TRENCH (N.W. end) taped out by Lt. FENWICK: work commenced with a strong working party, but not much progress made.	
" "	29th	–	Splinterproof shelter off CRUCIFIX ALLEY in front of LONGUEVAL excavated, and part of frames carried up.	
			C.T. from CRUCIFIX ALLEY to ANGLE TRENCH: 160 yards completed: 415 yards to depth of 4': 60× untouched.	

T2134. Wt. W708–776. 500000. 4/15. Sir J. C. & S.

Army Form C. 2118.

WAR DIARY
~~or~~
~~INTELLIGENCE SUMMARY~~.
(Erase heading not required.)

Instructions regarding War Diaries and Intelligence Summaries are contained in F. S. Regs., Part II. and the Staff Manual respectively. Title pages will be prepared in manuscript.

6th Field Coy R.E.

Place	Date	Hour	Summary of Events and Information	Remarks and references to Appendices
MAMETZ	30th	–	To DERNANCOURT	
DERNANCOURT	31st	–	To AIRAINES by tactical train	
			To BOISRAULT by march.	
			The necessity for an infantry party being attached to a Field Coy during operations was very noticeable: Sappers were being constantly employed on carrying stores, and were, ~~the~~ on arrival at site, often of little use for work.	
			Casualties amounted to 22 (of whom 3 were "slightly, at duty): representing about 20% of the men who actually worked in the front area.	
			[signature] Major R.E.	

T2134. Wt. W708–776. 500000. 4/15. Sir J. C. & S.

14 Div Vol 17

Army Form C. 2118.

WAR DIARY

~~or~~

~~INTELLIGENCE SUMMARY.~~

(Erase heading not required.)

Instructions regarding War Diaries and Intelligence Summaries are contained in F. S. Regs., Part II. and the Staff Manual respectively. Title pages will be prepared in manuscript.

61st Field Coy R.E.

Place	Date	Hour	Summary of Events and Information	Remarks and references to Appendices
	Sept			
BOISRAULT	1st–10th		Company training.	
			No 4 Section went to AULT on 4th to prepare rest camp, returning to BOISRAULT on 10th.	
	11th		To DERNANCOURT by tactical train.	
	13th		at DERNANCOURT.	
	14th		Dismounted to FRICOURT WOOD.	
			Mounted to BECORDEL.	
	15th		Dismounted to bivouac between MONTAUBAN and BERNAFAY WOOD: O.C. to DELVILLE WOOD at night to reconnoitre approaches to fighting line. 3 Killed, 9 wounded owing to explosion of a grenade (?).	
	16th		Company standing by all day. OC reconnoitred road through LONGUEVAL to about S.6.d. central with object of getting parties up, if necessary, across country from that point to firing line: sufficient wire etc collected just South of LONGUEVAL to wire in Brigade front, made up into loads and placed in dumps each containing 240x of entanglement. Brigade relieved during night 16/17.	
DERNANCOURT	17th–21st		Company did little beyond building a new store shed for XV Corps Signals at VIVIERS MILL. on 20th	Lieut Emmett to 62nd 2 Lieut Praun to 61st
	22nd		Company by bus to GROUCHES.	
GROUCHES	23rd–25th		General duties. OC to LE PERNONT and back on 24th.	
	26th		Company to HAUTEVILLE.	

T2134. Wt. W708—776. 500000. 4/15. Sir J. C. & S.

Instructions regarding War Diaries and Intelligence Summaries are contained in F. S. Regs., Part II. and the Staff Manual respectively. Title pages will be prepared in manuscript.

WAR DIARY

~~or~~

~~INTELLIGENCE SUMMARY.~~

(Erase heading not required.)

Army Form C. 2118.

61st Field Coy R.E.

Place	Date	Hour	Summary of Events and Information	Remarks and references to Appendices
	27th		Company, less transport and No 2 Section, to LE FERMONT; taking over of "F" Sector completed.	
			Transport to LARBRET. No 2 Section to LARBRET to take over Workshops and Park.	
LE FERMONT	28th–30th		Company employed on following:- Dugouts for M G Emplacements V1, V2, V3, V4, V5, V6, & THE MOUND	
			Dugouts near junctions S.F.T & FOREST STREET, SFT & FISH STREET	
			Russian Saps No 6. 7. 10. 12.	
			Survey of FACTORY POST completed.	
			Record list, giving details of all dugouts in sector, commenced.	
			Company has charge of two dumps for R.E. Stores. System of distribution of Stores through Staff Captain discontinued as from 1st October, all indents from units coming direct to R.E. Company.	
			Transport stood all moves very well.	
			Corpl Richards awarded D.C.M. for gallantry in DELVILLE WOOD on 18th Aug.	

E.M. Lees
Major RE
O.C. 61st Fd Coy RE

Army Form C. 2118.

Vol 18

Instructions regarding War Diaries and Intelligence Summaries are contained in F. S. Regs., Part II. and the Staff Manual respectively. Title pages will be prepared in manuscript.

WAR DIARY
or
INTELLIGENCE SUMMARY.

(*Erase heading not required.*)

Place	Date	Hour	Summary of Events and Information	Remarks and references to Appendices
			War Diary	
			of the	
			61st Field Coy R.E.	
			from 1st October 1916 to 31st October 1916.	
			[signature] Major R.E.	

T2134. Wt. W708-776. 500000. 4/15. Sir J. C. & S.

Instructions regarding War Diaries and Intelligence Summaries are contained in F. S. Regs., Part II. and the Staff Manual respectively. Title pages will be prepared in manuscript.

WAR DIARY

~~or~~

~~INTELLIGENCE SUMMARY~~.

(*Erase heading not required.*)

Army Form C. 2118.

61st Field Coy R.E.

Place	Date	Hour	Summary of Events and Information	Remarks and references to Appendices
LE FERMONT	—	—	The company (less one section employed at the LARBRET Workshops) was in LE FERMONT throughout the month. There are no events of importance to record – the company being employed mainly on R.E. work of the usual type – i.e. dugouts, M.G. emplacements, trench Tramways: the progress of these works was considerably hindered by the installation of accessories – this work used up large numbers of Sappers, especially as, owing to the wet weather, parapets collapsed in every direction.	

E.M. Lee
Major R.E.

T2134. Wt. W708–776. 500000. 4/15. Sir J. C. & S.

Army Form C. 2118.

Instructions regarding War Diaries and Intelligence Summaries are contained in F. S. Regs., Part II. and the Staff Manual respectively. Title pages will be prepared in manuscript.

WAR DIARY
or
INTELLIGENCE SUMMARY.
(Erase heading not required.)

Vol 19

Place	Date	Hour	Summary of Events and Information	Remarks and references to Appendices
			<u>Confidential</u> War Diary of 61st Fd Coy R.E. from 1st November 1916 to 30th November 1916. Volume X	

1577 Wt. W10791/1773 500,000 1/15 D. D. & L. A.D.S.S./Forms/C. 2118.

Instructions regarding War Diaries and Intelligence Summaries are contained in F. S. Regs., Part II. and the Staff Manual respectively. Title pages will be prepared in manuscript.

WAR DIARY
or
~~INTELLIGENCE SUMMARY.~~
(Erase heading not required.)

Army Form C. 2118.

SECRET 1

61st Coy R E

Place	Date	Hour	Summary of Events and Information	Remarks and references to Appendices
LE FERMONT	Nov. 1st – 4th		3 Sections F Sector 1 Section LARBRET (workshops)	
			150 Infantry and 12 sappers from 63rd Coy RE attached for special work on dug-outs from 2nd inst.	
			Work generally consisted of fixing new pattern firesteps throughout the F Sector front, extending and maintaining the tramway system, and constructing deep dug-outs: progress was good, the supply of materials being excellent.	
	5th		Company, having handed over to 87th Fd Coy R.E, moved from LEFERMONT to GOUY-EN-ARTOIS – a detachment of 12 men, with 1 officer, being left at LARBRET.	
GOUY-EN-ARTOIS	6th – 22nd		Company training, fieldworks, reports on increase of accommodation etc in GRAND RULLECOURT, SOMBRIN, and HAUTEVILLE, 41st Bde Fieldworks School, and various small jobs	
	23rd		Company from GOUY-EN-ARTOIS to ARRAS, for work with 12th & 35th Divisions.	
ARRAS.	24th – 30th		½ company, with 1 batt Inf, working in K. Sector under 35th Division – 5 dug-outs, tramway, & Trench 40	
			½ company, with ½ batt Inf, working in H. Sector under 12th Division – 2 dug-outs, various short lengths of C.T, and the Support line	
			Progress in K Sector fair – bad weather against really good progress with Tramway & Trench 40	
			Progress in H Sector bad – supply of stores very bad.	

E.M. Leis[?]
Major RE
O.C. 61st Fd Coy RE
1. 12. 16

1577 Wt. W10791/1773 500,000 1/15 D. D. & L. A.D.S.S./Forms/C. 2118.

Instructions regarding War Diaries and Intelligence Summaries are contained in F. S. Regs., Part II. and the Staff Manual respectively. Title pages will be prepared in manuscript.

WAR DIARY
or
INTELLIGENCE SUMMARY
(*Erase heading not required.*)

December 1916 –

Vol 20

61st Co. RE

Army Form C. 2118.

Place	Date	Hour	Summary of Events and Information	Remarks and references to Appendices
ARRAS	1st–7th		Nos I & III Sections employed as below in H SECTOR:-	
			(1). HAVANNAH ST. from Support to Front line, completed except for 50 yards, trench boarded on piles, revetted where necessary, deepened to 6 ft – 7 ft –	
			(2). HULLUCH ST, as for HAVANNAH ST except entirely completed –	
			(3). SUPPORT LINE from HAZEBROUCK ST to left of Sector – Fire steps made, deepened, trench boarded on piles, revetted where necessary –	
			(4) Only 1 days work done on the 2 dugouts due to lack of mine setts –	
			(5). HAYMARKET ST. Commenced deepening & trench boarding –	
			Nos II & IV Sections employed as below in I. SECTOR:-	
			(1). Trench 40:- From MONDAY AVE to LILLE ROAD – Completed except for a little levelling of parapet – Fire steps put in, traverses erected, trench deepened –	
			(2). Tramway:- 400 yards of track laid, all curves had to be bent by hand on site and this delayed laying very considerably – Trench cleared up to LAWRENCE AVE –	
			(3). 5 Dugouts – Progress varied from 2 ft 6 ins to 3 4 ft –	
	8th		Company moved to LIGNEREUILL –	

1577 Wt. W10791/1773 500,000 1/15 D. D. & L. A.D.S.S./Forms/C. 2118.

Army Form C. 2118.

Instructions regarding War Diaries and Intelligence Summaries are contained in F. S. Regs., Part II. and the Staff Manual respectively. Title pages will be prepared in manuscript.

WAR DIARY
or
INTELLIGENCE SUMMARY

(Erase heading not required.)

December 1916

Hour, Date, Place	Summary of Events and Information	Remarks and references to Appendices
LIGNEREUILL – 8th to 15th –	Drill, Box Respirators fitted, general "brush-up" –	
	Officers on Accomodation report of villages –	
13th –	2nd Lieut. E.R. FOSTER and No I Section moved to LARBRET and took over workshops & Park from 62nd Fd. Coy R.E. –	
15th –	Coy. marched to GOUY-EN-ARTOIS –	
16th.	Nos II, III & IV, & Hq. Sections moved to LE FERMONT (F Sector) and transport to LARBRET –	
18th – 30th	Work taken over from 87th Fd. Coy R.E. (i). RUSSIAN SAPS (ii). NISSEN HUTS at LE FERMONT. (iii). Repair of RIVIERE – WAILLY ROAD – New work commenced – (i). Bde. Hq Dugout – (ii). Dugout in SFT. (iii). " in RESERVE LINE. (iv) " in FARROW ST – (v). " for Left Bn. Hq.	
26th – 27th –	With the aid of the Pioneers 4 RUSSIAN SAPS were opened and T Heads established in one night working in 3 reliefs – Posts had been previously mined by the Infantry –	

1247 W 3299 200,000 (E) 8/14 J.B.C. & A. Forms/C. 2118/11.

Instructions regarding War Diaries and Intelligence Summaries are contained in F. S. Regs., Part II. and the Staff Manual respectively. Title pages will be prepared in manuscript.

WAR DIARY
or
INTELLIGENCE SUMMARY.
(Erase heading not required.)

Army Form C. 2118.

December 1916.

Place	Date	Hour	Summary of Events and Information	Remarks and references to Appendices
LE FERMONT.	31st		Consequent on the exceptionally bad weather and shelling the FRONT LINE had by this date got into a very bad condition – Hence the B.G.C. put this Coy in sole charge of its repair with the Bn in Reserve as a working party – This work was commenced on the 31st and all other work stopped except on RUSSIAN SAPS –	
			Personal :–	
	2.12.16		Major E.F.W. LEES ~~Dept~~ appointed to take charge of the Brigade ~~Depot~~ School, First Army –	
	2.12.16		~~Captain~~ Captain E.E.V. TEMPERLEY R.E. (S.R.) appointed O.C. –	
	5.12.16		Lieut. P. G. NOTTAGE R.E. (T.C.) ~~[illegible]~~ appointed 2nd in command from the 89th Fd Coy R.E. & reported from leave on 17.12.16.	
			E. E. V. Temperley Major R.E.(S.R.) O.C. 91st Fd Coy R.E. 1.1.17	

T2134. Wt. W708–776. 500000. 4/15. Sir J. C. & S.

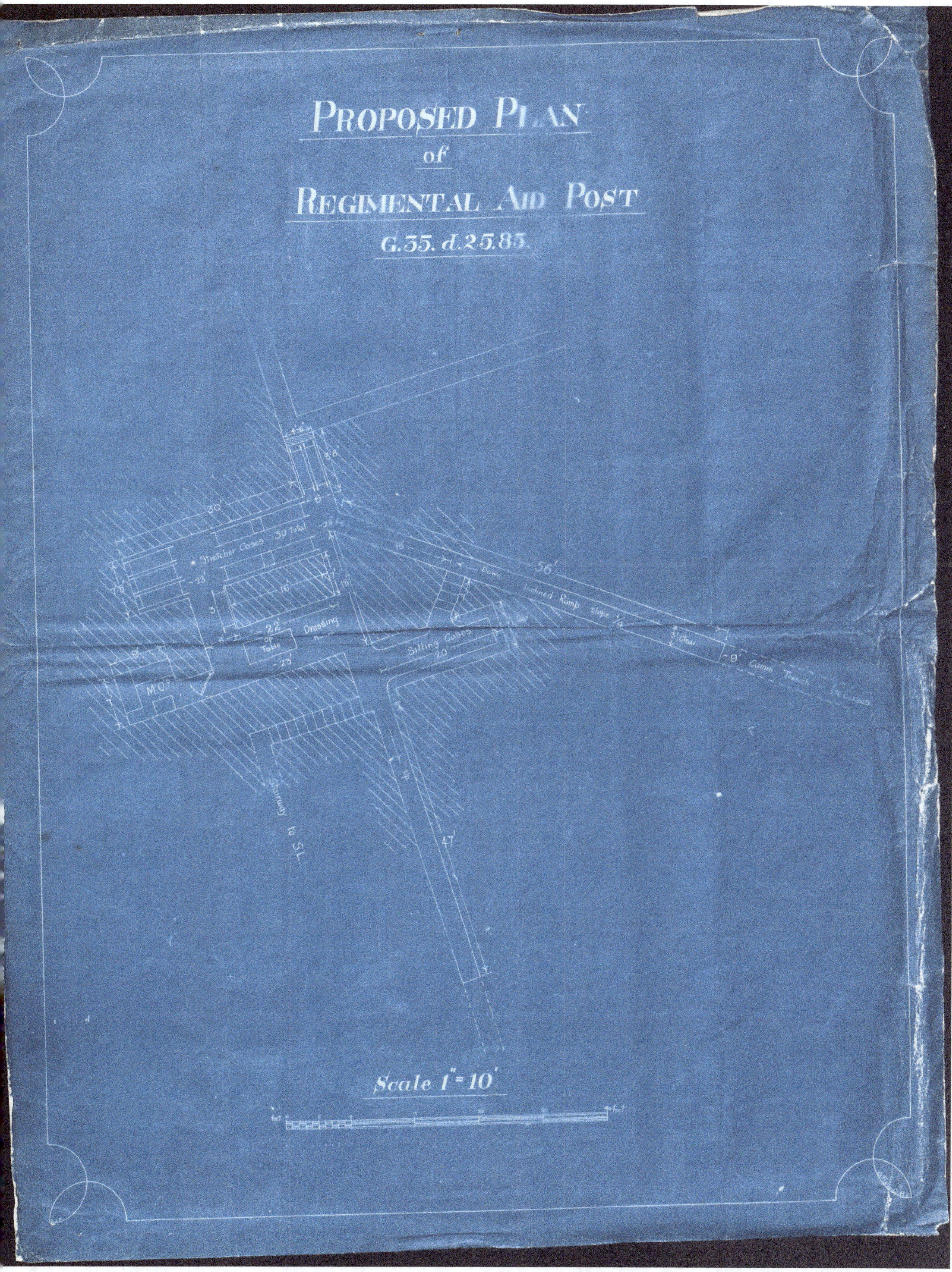

PROPOSED PLAN
of
REGIMENTAL AID POST
G.35. d.25.85.
Stretcher Cases
30 total
Dressing
Table
M.O's
Sitting Cases
Down
Inclined Ramp slope 1/4
56'
3' Clear
9'
Comm Trench
Stairway to S.L.
Up
47'
Scale 1" = 10'

Instructions regarding War Diaries and Intelligence Summaries are contained in F. S. Regs., Part II. and the Staff Manual respectively. Title pages will be prepared in manuscript.

WAR DIARY
or
INTELLIGENCE SUMMARY. 61st Fd Coy R.E.

(Erase heading not required.)

Army Form C. 2118.

Vol 21

Place	Date	Hour	Summary of Events and Information January . 1917 –	Remarks and references to Appendices
LEFERMONT	E		The FRONT LINE was worked on and made passable and No 3 Sect was taken	
F Sector –			off on the 7th, No 4 Sect on the 10th, and No 1 Sect on the 15th and put on	
			their normal work –	
	11th		No 2 Sectn relieved No 1 Sect at LARBRET –	
	15th		One section from the 62nd Fd Coy R.E. and the 89th Fd Coy R.E. arrived to assist in the	
			building of Trench Mortar Emplacements –	
	23rd		These two sections returned to their units –	
			Seven new Medium Trench Mortar Emplacements and Bomb Stores were built	
			by them and Three old M.T.M. Emplacements were reclaimed – Splinter proof cover	
			for the Emplacements and for the Bomb Stores were provided –	
			Also Three Heavy Trench Emplacements and Splinter Proof Shelters were built by	
			them and one by the No 4 Sect –	
			For the remainder of the month the Company was employed on	
			(1). Dugouts, new mined –	
			(2). Strengthening old Dugouts in the line.	
			(3). 230 yards of Tramway laid between WAILLY DUMP & SOMERSET HOUSE –	

T2134. Wt. W708–776. 500000. 4/15. Sir J. C. & S.

Instructions regarding War Diaries and Intelligence Summaries are contained in F. S. Regs., Part II. and the Staff Manual respectively. Title pages will be prepared in manuscript.

WAR DIARY
or
INTELLIGENCE SUMMARY.
(Erase heading not required.)

61st Fd. Coy. R.E.

Army Form C. 2118.

Place	Date	Hour	Summary of Events and Information January 1917	Remarks and references to Appendices
			(4). Fixing gas curtains –	
			(5). Portable O.Ps. –	
			(6) Road Repair –	
			(7) Bde Canteen –	
			(8). Repairing S.A.A. & Bomb Store near BREWERY DUMP –	
			Personal:–	
			act. Capt. E.E.V. TEMPERLEY RE.SR appointed acting Major – 2.12.16.	
			Lieut. P. J. NOTTAGE R.E. " " Capt. 5.12.16.	
			E. C. V. Temperley MAJOR R. E. (S. R.) O. C. 61st FIELD COY, R. E. 1.2.17.	

T2134. Wt. W708–776. 500000. 4/15. Sir J. C. & S.

WAR DIARY
or
INTELLIGENCE SUMMARY.
(Erase heading not required.)

Instructions regarding War Diaries and Intelligence Summaries are contained in F. S. Regs., Part II. and the Staff Manual respectively. Title pages will be prepared in manuscript.

Army Form C. 2118.

61 Fd Coy RE

Vol 22

Place	Date	Hour	Summary of Events and Information February 1917	Remarks and references to Appendices
LE FERMONT	~~3rd~~ 2nd		No 3 Section relieved No 2 Section at LARBRET PARK.	
	3rd		Handed over to 57th Fd. Coy. R.E.	
			No 2 Section moved to WARLUS to work under C.R.E.	
			Hqs. & Nos 1 & 4 Section moved to ARRAS –	
	5th		½ No 1 Sectn to DAINVILLE.	
	6th		Commenced work in H2 Sector –	
	5th		No 3 Section moved to DAINVILLE and took over Divl workshops from 11th Kings.	
ARRAS	5th – 28th		The work in H2 Sector consisted of	
			Trench Tramming – 60 cm. from R.E. DUMP to SUPPORT LINE.	
			Bn Hq. Dugout	
			Dressing Station Dugout.	
			Repairs to old Dugouts.	
			Erection of Sylvid Pattern Shelters.	
			The only work of especial interest was the Dressing Stn. – A blue print of this is attached –	
			The through passage and the stepped entrances were part of old mine galleries and	
			the Dressing station was made off this –	

E. C. [illegible]
MAJOR R.E. (S.R.)
O. C. 61st FIELD COY, R.E.
1·3·17.

T2134. Wt. W708–776. 500000. 4/15. Sir J. C. & S.

Army Form C. 2118.

61 F Co RE
14 Div
Vol 23

Instructions regarding War Diaries and Intelligence Summaries are contained in F. S. Regs., Part II. and the Staff Manual respectively. Title pages will be prepared in manuscript.

WAR DIARY
or
INTELLIGENCE SUMMARY.
(Erase heading not required.)

March 1917.

Place	Date	Hour	Summary of Events and Information	Remarks and references to Appendices
ARRAS	1st–18th		Work continued on following works by Nos 4 and majority of No 1 Sectn.	
			Trench Tramway – 60 cm – Work much delayed by trench badly falling in due to wet & frost.	
			Bn. Hq. Dugout – completed –	
			Dummy Station	
			Fixing Camouflage O.P.S.	
	1st–18th		No 2 Section on Divisional Work under C.R.E.	
			No 3 " at Divisional Workshops & Parks –	
			½ No 1 " ditto –	
	18th		The Enemy evacuated his front line system & fell back on the COJEUL SWITCH –	
	18th–20th		Bridging trenches to allow horse transport –	
	20th		No 2 Sectn rejoined the Company.	
	23rd		No 3 " " " "	
			During this month preparations for the offensive were continually carried out – Forward dumps sited and stocked, water tanks	

T2134. Wt. W708–776. 500000. 4/15. Sir J. C. & S.

Instructions regarding War Diaries and Intelligence Summaries are contained in F. S. Regs., Part II. and the Staff Manual respectively. Title pages will be prepared in manuscript.

WAR DIARY
or
INTELLIGENCE SUMMARY.
(*Erase heading not required.*)

Army Form C. 2118.

Place	Date	Hour	Summary of Events and Information	Remarks and references to Appendices
			erected and rendered splinter proof, tramway carried forward to the enemy front line, trench bridges made & carried up, battle stores collected — On the 24th the 42nd & 43rd Bdes handed over the line to the 41st Bde and on the 29th the 87th Fd. Coy handed over to this Coy —	
	28th		Mill at ACHICOURT was demolished as it was used as a ranging mark by the enemy. The walls of the mill were 4 ft 6 ins thick at the point to be cut and the perimeter of the mill to be demolished was 30 ft. — 350 lbs of ammonal were placed in holes cut in the wall in tins of 50 lbs — 100 lbs were placed under a pile of bricks & timber in the centre of the mill — The charge was exploded electrically and the demolition as designed was complete — a few bricks were thrown some 600 yards —	
			Personal :-	
			~~Lieut~~ — E.V.M. CROFTON RE (S.R.) reported on 25.3.17	
			2nd Lieut. G.T.W. HERFORD RE arrived on probation for 1 month 2.3.17	
			2nd Lieut — N.S. CLOUSTON evacuated sick	

[signature]
MAJOR R.E. (S.R.)
O.C. 81st FIELD COY, R.E.

T2134. Wt. W708–776. 500000. 4/15. Sir J. C. & S.

SECRET

61 Fd Coy R.E.

Army Form C. 2118. 14

Vol 24

Instructions regarding War Diaries and Intelligence Summaries are contained in F. S. Regs., Part II. and the Staff Manual respectively. Title pages will be prepared in manuscript.

WAR DIARY
or
INTELLIGENCE SUMMARY.
(Erase heading not required.)

April 1917

Place	Date	Hour	Summary of Events and Information	Remarks and references to Appendices
1st to 7th inst –			On the night of 1st–2nd 41st Inf. Bde. was relieved by the 42 Inf Bde & the 43rd Inf. Bde.	
			During the period marginally stated following works were carried out :–	
			For 41st Inf. Bde	
			(I) Fixing water tanks for Reserve water.	
			(II) Supplying unit tools & stores to be carried ~~out~~ in the assault	
			(III) Preparing Bde Hqs in the CAVES	
			(IV) Preparing O.P. and Strutted Slit Trench – [I afterwards heard that the strutting saved the Intelligence Officer's life – a 5.9" shell caused the trench to fall in and buried this officer – the strutting gave him air space till dug out and prevented complete burial –]	
			For 42nd Inf. Bde	
			(I) Completing and revetting HALIFAX ST Gangway.	
			(II) " HUNTER ST Regl. Aid Post –	
			(III) Clearing out and framing enemy dugouts – 2 Bn Hqs., 1 Coy Hqs, 1 Bde Bomb Store provided –	
			(IV) Completing the fixing of Water tanks for Reserve Water in the trenches –	
			(V). Bridging trenches –	
			(VI) Providing cut & cover Dugout for dynamo and Engine at Bde Hqs –	

T2134. Wt. W708–776. 500000. 4/15. Sir J. C. & S.

Instructions regarding War Diaries and Intelligence Summaries are contained in F. S. Regs., Part II. and the Staff Manual respectively. Title pages will be prepared in manuscript.

WAR DIARY
or
INTELLIGENCE SUMMARY.
(Erase heading not required.)

Army Form C. 2118.

2

Place	Date	Hour	Summary of Events and Information April. 1917	Remarks and references to Appendices
			(vii) Forming Forward Battle Reserve of R.E. Stores –	
			(viii). Supplying Bde with Battle R.E. Stores to be carried over in assault –	
			(ix) Taping and arranging the digging of 3260 yds of Assembly Trench, 400 yards of Communication Trench in 3 nights with 1715 men –	
			43rd Inf. Bde 4a Bde advanced their line 750 yards on their right and 525 yards on their left –	
			(i) Fitting up old enemy dugout as a Regt. aid Post –	
			(ii) Repairing Water Tanks for Reserve Water –	
			(iii). Trench-boarding trenches & making trench boards –	
			(iv) Fixing notice boards to new trenches –	
			(v) Fixing bridges and marking overland routes	
			(vi). Making 6 Cut & Cover splinter proof dugouts for Bn Hqs. in new Assembly Trenches – Completed in 2 days.	
			(vii) Taping and arranging the digging of ~~[illegible]~~ 3730 yards of assembly Trench and 2650 yards of Communication Trench in 6 nights with 2025 men –	
			The 43rd Bde advanced their line 360 yards on their right and 420 yards on their left –	

T2134. Wt. W708–776. 500000. 4/15. Sir J. C. & S.

Instructions regarding War Diaries and Intelligence Summaries are contained in F. S. Regs., Part II. and the Staff Manual respectively. Title pages will be prepared in manuscript.

WAR DIARY
or
INTELLIGENCE SUMMARY.
(Erase heading not required.)

Army Form C. 2118.

Place	Date	Hour	Summary of Events and Information	Remarks and references to Appendices
			Not the least difficult of the above work was supplying the three Brigades with Stores and keeping in touch with each of them –	
	8.ᵃ		Completed certain works for the Bde –	
			HQs. and No 1 Section moved to forward dugouts, just West of BEAURAINS –	
	9.ᵃ		General Assault by THIRD ARMY on German system of defences –	
			Nos 1 & 3 Sect– moved up to forward dugouts before daybreak –	
			The work assigned to this Coy by the C.R.E. during operations was the laying of a 60 cm. DECAUVILLE tramway from a point some 1600 yards behind our Front assembly trench on the BEAURAINS – NEUVILLE VITASSE Road to join up with the enemy system of tramway leading to WANCOURT –	
			The assault of the 14ᵗʰ Div commenced at 7.30 a.m. and No 1 Section moved out from the dugouts at 9.15 a.m – The other sections followed at about 10.30 a m & 11.30 a m –	
			170 yards of track were laid and 1300 yards of line prepared for laying –	
			Work was much delayed by shelling and the difficulty of getting up track	

Instructions regarding War Diaries and Intelligence Summaries are contained in F. S. Regs., Part II. and the Staff Manual respectively. Title pages will be prepared in manuscript.

WAR DIARY
or
INTELLIGENCE SUMMARY.
(Erase heading not required.)

Army Form C. 2118.

Place	Date	Hour	Summary of Events and Information	Remarks and references to Appendices
			on the pontoon wagons owing to the congestion on the roads –	
	10th		1080 yards laid –	
	11th		550 yards "	
	12th		470 " " – All men were recalled from work at about 4 p.m. – Company moved to DAINVILLE –	
			A total of 2270 yards of track were laid in 3½ days work,	
			1170 " of old DECAUVILLE track was salved –	
			One Section was employed in salving & loading track, and three Sections in clearing the track and laying – Only 17 Inf as a loading party were available –	
			The enemy tramway system was found to have been almost completely destroyed up to a distance of 1600 yards from the enemy front line – Beyond this point about 95% of the track could be taken into use again –	
	13th		Company moved to BEAUMETZ –	
	15th		" " " LE CAUROY	

Instructions regarding War Diaries and Intelligence Summaries are contained in F. S. Regs., Part II. and the Staff Manual respectively. Title pages will be prepared in manuscript.

WAR DIARY
or
INTELLIGENCE SUMMARY.
(Erase heading not required.)

Army Form C. 2118.

Place	Date	Hour	Summary of Events and Information	Remarks and references to Appendices
	16th		Drill and Inspections of kit etc.	
	17th		Pontoon drill (rafts).	
	18th		Knots and lashings use of spars.	
	19th		Officers River Reconnaissance & bridging scheme, O.R Route March & Baths.	
	20th		Weldon Trestle, Rafts, Trestle Bridging	
	21st		——— ditto ———	
	22nd		Sunday: church parade in morning. no other parades.	
	23rd		Company from LE CAUROY to BIENVILLERS	
	24th		Company from BIENVILLERS to RANSART, thence to BLAIRVILLE.	
	25th		Company to shelters about 1 mile West of WANCOURT on WANCOURT - TILLOY Road.	Map
	26th to 30th		Constructing bridge for 18 prs over R. COJEUL at N.28.d.2.6. - completed.	51. B. S.W.2.
			Improvements to Brigade H.Q. in N.22.d.5.6. - one cut and cover shelter completed: some work on dug-outs.	
			Constructing shelter for stretcher cases & cookhouse at N.22.d.8.3 - completed.	
			Constructing shelters for stretcher cases at N.23.d.9.4 - in hand.	
			Constructing 3 cut and cover shelters for Battn H.Q. in O.19.c.2.8 - in hand.	
			Constructing shelters for company about 1500 yards W. of original bivouac - completed.	
			Additional accommodation for C.R.E and R.Q.	[signature] Major R.E. O.C. 61st F[ield] Co[y] R.E.

T2134. Wt. W708—776. 500000. 4/15. Sir J. C. & S.

A

14th Division.

Xth Corps. G.101/17/43.
14th Divn. G.S.903.

The Corps Commander wishes to express his appreciation of the work done by the Royal Engineers, Pioneer Battalion, and Infantry of the 14th Division on the Menin Road and PLUMER'S. DRIVE.

Despite the difficult conditions, the work of completing PLUMBER'S DRIVE, and opening up of the MENIN ROAD from HOOGE, has been rapidly done. The repairs to PUMBER'S DRIVE carried out on the night of 26th/27th October, reflect great credit on those concerned.

31/10/17.

sd/ A.R. CAMERON.
BRIGADIER - GENERAL.
GENERAL STAFF, XTH. CORPS.

O.C. 61st Field Company, R.E.

FOR INFORMATION.

I wish to thank all ranks of the company for the way they stuck to the work and finished the job.

1.11.1917.

D.S. Collins [illegible]

C.R.E. 14th (LIGHT) [illegible]

Confidential

Army Form C. 2118.

Instructions regarding War Diaries and Intelligence Summaries are contained in F. S. Regs., Part II. and the Staff Manual respectively. Title pages will be prepared in manuscript.

WAR DIARY
or
~~INTELLIGENCE SUMMARY.~~

(Erase heading not required.)

Vol 25

Place	Date	Hour	Summary of Events and Information	Remarks and references to Appendices
			War Diary of the 61st Field Coy RE 1st May 1917 — 31st May 1917.	
			[illegible signature] Major RE O.C. 61st Fd Coy RE	

1577 Wt. W10791/1773 500,000 1/15 D. D. & L. A.D.S.S./Forms/C. 2118.

Instructions regarding War Diaries and Intelligence Summaries are contained in F. S. Regs., Part II. and the Staff Manual respectively. Title pages will be prepared in manuscript.

WAR DIARY

or

~~INTELLIGENCE SUMMARY.~~

(*Erase heading not required.*)

Army Form C. 2118.

61st Field Coy R.E.

Place	Date MAY	Hour	Summary of Events and Information	Remarks and references to Appendices
ARRAS	1st	—	Constructing shelter for stretcher cases and cookhouse at N.22.d.8.3 – work completed	Map 51.B.S.W.
	2		Constructing 3 cut and cover shelters as Batt^n HQ in O.19.c.28: 3 chambers each 10'x7', framed with 9x3 – roof 5x2 girders, 1' centre to centre, and C.I.: bursting layer of rails and C.I.: chambers connected with fire trench and with each other: more than this could not be done in the time: there were no direct hits during the battle, but several very near, and the shelters stood.	
			Continued construction of UP and DOWN bridge for 'A' class traffic over R. COJEUL N.29.a.5.8.	
	3rd		General attack – not a success.	
			Company wiring at night – no start possible until after midnight – task set carried through, but wire knocked about as soon as put up.	
	4th/13th		Constructing defensive line from N.16 Central to N 22 c.3.5. 1 Coy Pioneers attached. Line wired with 2 belts of low wire and 18' wide, and an apron fence: latter not completed before handing work over to 83rd Coy R.E.: Strong points wired all round, also M.G.E.A.: gaps marked.	
			Five strong points dug and completed.	
			Shelters for garrisons of No 1 and 2 S.P's completed.	
			Shelter for M.G. Det (B) completed, for M.G. Det (A) half completed, for M.G. Det (D) commenced – all "cut and cover" with bursting layer	
			Tunnelled shelter for M.G. Det (C) – entrances completed – chamber 1/3rd done.	

1577 Wt. W10791/1773 500,000 1/15 D. D. & L. A.D.S.S./Forms/C. 2118.

Instructions regarding War Diaries and Intelligence Summaries are contained in F. S. Regs., Part II. and the Staff Manual respectively. Title pages will be prepared in manuscript.

WAR DIARY
or
~~INTELLIGENCE SUMMARY.~~
(Erase heading not required.)

Army Form C. 2118.

Place	MAY Date	Hour	Summary of Events and Information	Remarks and references to Appendices
ARRAS.	4th/13th	(continued)	Work across WANCOURT valley frequently interrupted by shelling.	
			Bridges "UP" and "DOWN" for A Class traffic over R. COJEUL (N.29.a.5.8) completed on 9th — approaches require making up, and decking on "DOWN" bridge should be strengthened: seven 8¾" x 5" girders, found in German dump in WANCOURT, used in each bridge.	
			Sawing pickets for wire entanglements — 15,000 sawn.	
			Building additional accommodation for 41st Inf Bde.	
	14th/24th		41st Inf Bde in the line: work throughout the period proceeded slowly: shelling fairly persistent, and a good deal of gas: on two nights no work was possible.	
			(New) EGRET TRENCH from about N.30 Central to N.30.b.9.7 constructed: firesteps revetted in 27 firebays: R.E. and infantry working parties.	
			MALLARD TRENCH from about O.25.a.6.6. to O.25.b.8.2 commenced: R.E. and infantry.	
			Two belts of low wire erected in front of new EGRET: saps marked.	
			One belt of low wire erected in front of MALLARD for 600 yards N. of road O.25.a.6.3	
			Digging FOSTER AVENUE from ALBATROSS to Rt. Batt. HQ: fair progress: RE and infantry.	
			Commenced cut and cover shelter for stretchers at Rt. Batt. HQ.	
			Sawing pickets.	
			Infantry working parties generally worked badly: every night it was necessary to detail a considerable number of sappers to accompany the working parties.	
			A trench board factory, manned by pioneers from various battalions, was worked throughout	

WAR DIARY

or

~~INTELLIGENCE SUMMARY.~~

(Erase heading not required.)

Army Form C. 2118.

Instructions regarding War Diaries and Intelligence Summaries are contained in F. S. Regs., Part II. and the Staff Manual respectively. Title pages will be prepared in manuscript.

61st Fd Coy RE

Place	MAY Date	Hour	Summary of Events and Information	Remarks and references to Appendices
ARRAS.	14th/24th		this period: about 800 were made by 18 men, who had to do their own salving in RONVILLE and BEAURAINS, no other material being available.	
	25th/31st		The company remained up when the 41st Bde went out: one night lost through heavy rains.	
			LION switch commenced – about half completed on 31st – RE and infantry.	
			Wiring (2 belts of low wire) LION trench from SHIKAR to LION switch, and LION switch from LION to PANTHER.	
			It was not possible to get more than 90 – 100 men per night from the Bde, so work did not progress as it should have.	
			A Field works Class for officers and N.C.O's of the 41st Bde was held, commencing on the 29th with laying out, digging, revetting, and floorboarding trenches, and constructing wire entanglements were carried out.	
			4 sappers employed for 3 weeks on the Reserve Bde Camp.	
			Weather very good – health of company only fair.	

[signature]
Major RE
OC. 61st Fd Coy RE

1577 Wt. W10791/1773 500,000 1/15 D. D. & L. A.D.S.S./Forms/C. 2118.

CONFIDENTIAL.

14th Division "A"

Herewith War Diary of 61st Fd. Co. R.E. for the month of June '17.

[signature] Lt & Adjt R.E.
for Lieut Colonel. R.E.
C.R.E. 14th Division.

4.7.17.

Vol 26

Army Form C. 2118.

Instructions regarding War Diaries and Intelligence Summaries are contained in F. S. Regs., Part II. and the Staff Manual respectively. Title pages will be prepared in manuscript.

WAR DIARY

~~or~~

~~INTELLIGENCE SUMMARY.~~

(Erase heading not required.)

61st Fd Coy R.E.

Place	Date JUNE	Hour	Summary of Events and Information	Remarks and references to Appendices
ARRAS.	1st – 9th	—	Company employed on "A" line in front of WANCOURT between R. COJEUL and road in 0.25 a 0.7. Line wired, but no firebays, when taken over, except for 7 partially dug in LION Switch. The following work was completed by the morning of the 9th (nights of 31st/1st and 3rd/4th lost, owing to heavy rain in first instance and Brigade Relief in second instance). LION Switch – 12 firebays – completed. * LION trench – 8 firebays completed. * EGRET trench between SHIKAR and KESTRAL – 21 firebays completed. * EGRET trench between KESTRAL and 0.25 a 0.7. – 10 firebays completed. * trench itself requires widening and deepening to act as a "command" trench. Wire in front of LION Switch and LION thickened. An additional belt of wire, 18' thick, erected in front of EGRET between KESTREL and 0.25. a. 0.7 Gaps in wire marked along whole "A" line by white posts. Working parties varied from 100 to 190 men per night: in addition 100 Pioneers were made available on 3 nights – weather fine throughout.	Map. 51. B. S.W. Sketch of firebay. ← 24' → 5' 4' 15'
	9th		Company moved to AGNY	
	11th		" " " MONCHIET	
	12th		" " " GAUDIEMPRE.	
	13th		" " " LOUVENCOURT.	
	14th–16th		Kit etc. Inspections & drill.	

1577 Wt. W10791/1773 500,000 1/15 D. D. & L. A.D.S.S./Forms/C. 2118.

Army Form C. 2118.

Instructions regarding War Diaries and Intelligence Summaries are contained in F. S. Regs., Part II. and the Staff Manual respectively. Title pages will be prepared in manuscript.

WAR DIARY
or
~~INTELLIGENCE SUMMARY.~~
(Erase heading not required.)

Place	Date	Hour	Summary of Events and Information	Remarks and references to Appendices
	17th		Dismounted portion of Coy. moved to ORVILLE to do a 4 days course of bridging –	
			Stores sorted, wagons unloaded, practised knots & lashings, making trestles –	
	18th – 21st		Bridging course, including light pile bridging, trestle (Service & lashed) bridging, pontooning –	
	22nd		Coy. returned to LOUVENCOURT	
	23rd – 27th.		Training, firing course on miniature range.	
			A certain number of small works were carried out for C.R.E. & Bdes –	
			Also ~~any~~ two field works courses for 41st Inf. Bde. were held –	
	27th		C.R.E.'s Inspection –	
	28th		Coy marched to SAULTY and entrained –	
	29th		Detrained at BAILLEUL and marched to camp near LOCRE –	
	~~[illegible]~~		Received instructions for work on Corps line from C.R.E. IX Corps Troops –	
	30th		Coy marched to camp near VIERSTRAAT –	

E. S. U. Temple(?) (?)
Major R.E.
O.C. 61st Fd. Coy. R.E.
30.6.17.

1577 Wt. W10791/1773 500,000 1/15 D. D. & L. A.D.S.S./Forms/C. 2118.

Instructions regarding War Diaries and Intelligence Summaries are contained in F. S. Regs., Part II. and the Staff Manual respectively. Title pages will be prepared in manuscript.

WAR DIARY
or
INTELLIGENCE SUMMARY.
(Erase heading not required.)

Vol 27 Army Form C. 2118.

61st Field Coy R.E.

Place	Date	Hour	JULY Summary of Events and Information	Remarks and references to Appendices
VIERSTRAT	1st - 30th		The whole Company worked throughout this period on the RIDGE DEFENCES some 1000 yards North-East of WYTSCHAETE – These Defences consisted of Front and Support lines connected by communication trenches – Owing to the wet state of the soil only a 4 ft trench could be dug in places and this meant a great expenditure of labour in banking up – Revetting:– The whole system had to be revetted throughout – The type of revetting ordered to be used by the Corps proved laborious and consisted of the following arrangement – a 3 ft U frame was placed in the trench and the sides revetted with corrugated iron and above this X.P.M. panels were used to revet the sides and were anchored back with 6 ft angle iron pickets – Wiring:– Type adopted was 8 to 12 rows of a very much spread out apron thus giving a belt of wire from 50 to 100 yards deep. This system gave practically complete invisibility at about 300 yards and no doubt would not show up on aeroplane photographs.	

1577 Wt. W10791/1773 500,000 1/15 D. D. & L. A.D.S.S./Forms/C. 2118.

Instructions regarding War Diaries and Intelligence Summaries are contained in F. S. Regs., Part II. and the Staff Manual respectively. Title pages will be prepared in manuscript.

WAR DIARY
or
INTELLIGENCE SUMMARY.
(*Erase heading not required.*)

Army Form C. 2118.

Place	Date	Hour	Summary of Events and Information	Remarks and references to Appendices
			JULY.	
			Working Party:- 100 Inf were available for work and were supplied by 11th WARWICKS (37th Div.) from the 3rd to 15th and by the 8th K.R.R.C. from 15th to 30th.-	
			Work done:- During this period following work was done -	
			500 yards of Front Line completed with a few shelters -	
			170 " " Communication Trench do	
			50 " " " " dug	
			4200 yards run of apron wire in belts of 25 yards -	
			110 yards of German trench repaired but not completed - (Pioneers also worked on this) -	
			The work was quite appreciably retarded by shelling -	
	31st		General attack round YPRES Salient took place. Stood by in camp -	
			Personnel:-	
	14th		Lieut E.V.M. CROFTON R.E.(S.R.) killed	
	14th		2nd Lieut R.C. STRONNER R.E. (T.C.) reported for duty -	
	20th		2nd Lieut W. C. ELTOFF R.E. (T.C.) reported for duty -	

E. C. [signature]
MAJOR R.E. (S.R.)
O. C. 61st FIELD COY. R.E.
31.7.17.

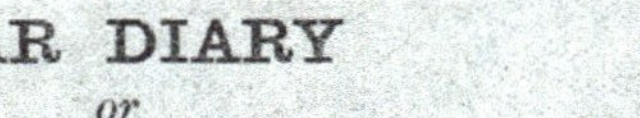

Instructions regarding War Diaries and Intelligence Summaries are contained in F. S. Regs., Part II. and the Staff Manual respectively. Title pages will be prepared in manuscript.

WAR DIARY
or
INTELLIGENCE SUMMARY.
(*Erase heading not required.*)

Army Form C. 2118.

Vol 28

Place	Date	Hour	Summary of Events and Information — AUGUST —	Remarks and references to Appendices
VIERSTRAT	1st–5th		Waiting for orders in camp. Time occupied by drill, inspections etc – Very wet weather –	
	6th		Marched to new billets 1 mile north of CAESTRE –	
CAESTRE	6th–14th		This period occupied by inspections, drill, WELDON trestle, use of spars, map reading and demolitions – This period proved extremely useful in seeing to the Coy equipment and general improvement of discipline —	
	15th		Moved to WIPPONHOEK area, attached to 43rd Bde Group –	
WIPPONHOEK	16th		Drill etc –	
	17th		Moved to 28 H29 b 8.6 as the Division was somewhat unexpectedly called upon to take over from the 56th Div who were rather severely handled in their attack of the 17th –	
	18th		Day spent in reconnoitring the line of the offensive – Situation a little hazy and utterly unorganized – No proper tracks up to the line exist – No line behind the front line – Owing to the Brigade boundary being parallel more or less to the front line it is very difficult to organize the defence in depth –	
	19th		Nos 1 & 2 Sections began work on trench board track from Zillebeke, N. of Dormy Ho, & Maple Copse to Sanctuary Wood, (Stirling Castle & Clapham Junct) 5am till noon. No 4 Section taking over at noon. The work was continued next day, but little was achieved as a heavy Enemy barrage was put down, as retaliation for our Smoke barrage. No 4 Section were working in the wood & suffered one casualty.	
	20th			

1577 Wt. W10791/1773 500,000 1/15 D. D. & L. A.D.S.S./Forms/C. 2118.

Instructions regarding War Diaries and Intelligence Summaries are contained in F. S. Regs., Part II. and the Staff Manual respectively. Title pages will be prepared in manuscript.

WAR DIARY
or
INTELLIGENCE SUMMARY.
(Erase heading not required.)

Army Form C. 2118.

Place	Date	Hour	August. Summary of Events and Information	Remarks and references to Appendices
WIPPENHOEK	20th Cont.		At 5 am. 2 carrying parties (each 250 strong) rendezvoused at DORMY HO & ZILLEBEKE CH. respectively to take stores to forward dumps at Stirling Castle & Clapham Junct. At dawn Zillebeke was being shelled & the traffic on the road (pack animals w/ ammunition & our 2 pontoon wagons w/ R.E. stores) were held up for some time. They got through just before the sun rose. One pack animal was killed & lay on the road side still steaming from his exertions, besides others killed on previous days. The valley was filled w/ mist, but whether gas or not it was difficult to determine – a little tear gas!	
"	21st		No 1 & 2 on Stirling Castle & Clapham Junction — tracks. Good days work but suffered 3 casualties – sapper Smith killed. Lt Eltoft marked out track from Stirling's Castle to Menin Rd.. No 4 on track in the afternoon. No 3 on both days working at track on Observation Ridge, wh. fortunately was not shelled during the hours of work although Sanctuary wood on one side & Fosse Wood on the other were heavily shelled.	
"	22nd		Attack by the 42nd & 43rd Inf Bdes. No work for the sappers. A party composed of Cpl Harvey & 6 sappers waited in concrete dug-out in Sanctuary wood for 12 hours in readiness for demolition work wh. the infantry might require in their advance. The demolition party was not called for. They were severely shelled all day, but suffered no casualties. No 3 began work strutting Dormy Ho. (Bde Hq 43rd) wh. had been repeatedly hit during the day.	
"	23rd		No 3 carried on w/ work at Dormy ho & started work on Gunners-Dugouts, (82nd Bde RFA) 200x N. of Dormy Ho. Lt Eltoft, Cpl Harvey & 2 sappers to meet RAMC working party at 5.30 am. at Culvert, Menin Rd.. They were delayed by barrage & reached the rendezvous 10 minutes late, but working party w/ unable to [illegible] through barrage. No 1 returned to camp from dugouts No 2 "stood by".	
"	24th		Work was cancelled.	
"	25th		Began work (No 1 & 3) round Zillebeke Lake, made small bridge & fascine track, No 2 section completed artillery dug-out, 30ft repaired.	
Busseboom	26th		Moved to camp on Ouderdom – Poperinghe Rd. Fine weather for marching, men in good spirits. Torrential rain set in about 10 pm. rained all night.	
"	27th		In camp raining all day	
	28th		do. weather fine. Received orders to stand by for moving on the 29th to Berthen Area to join 2nd Army (2nd Anzac Corps)	
	29th		do weather showery: cleaned up as we left camp at 4 pm. Marched thro' Reninghelst, Westoutre, over Mt Noir through La Manche to "Ferme Rouge" wh. we reached at 9 pm.. Delay caused by motor lorries & the 41st Bde.	
	30-31st		At "Ferme Rouge" (Berthen Area) Coy. Training after improving amenities of camp. Section drill. Lecture by M.O.	

[signature] Capt RE. 31/8/17
a/OC 81st Fld Coy RE.

Instructions regarding War Diaries and Intelligence Summaries are contained in F. S. Regs., Part II. and the Staff Manual respectively. Title pages will be prepared in manuscript.

WAR DIARY
or
INTELLIGENCE SUMMARY.
(Erase heading not required.)

Army Form C. 2118.

Vol 29

Place	Date	Hour	Summary of Events and Information Sept.	Remarks and references to Appendices
Berthen Area.	1st to 4th		The Coy. Remained at "Ferme Rouge" from 9pm on the evening of 29th Aug till the morning of 4th Sept. when we moved to a camp near Neuve Eglise which was reached in the afternoon of 4th. The work allotted to the 61st Coy. was to construct a duck-board track from a point where the Messines road became obliterated, to an aid-post at Swaynes Farm & to make an Infantry track from Wulverghem to Middle farm. Swaynes Farm & Middle Farm are both on the Wytschaete, Messines Rd & lie a few hundred yards to the N of Wulverghem Rd to Messines.	
Neuve Eglise	5th		I met Evans (O.C. 43rd F.A.) at 5 am on the road outside the camp & went by car to Boyles Farm. The sun rose over the Messines Ridge as we walked up the hill towards the village of that name & showed the country on both sides of us. Although it is desolate enough yet there is plenty of green & the trees are not so skatchy as in SANCTUARY wood. The morning was spent reconnoitering.	
	6th		Lt Stronner with 2 sections & party of 25 R.A.M.C. began work at 5.30 am on the duck board track. They were relieved at 9.30 am. by No 1 section. No 4 section at 9.30 am began work on the mule track (Lt Pram) with 20 men of 8th K.R.R.C.. He was relieved at 1.30 by No 3 section.	
	7th		Work as on the 6th except that Lt Stronner & his section began work at 9.30 am & were relieved at 1.30 pm. He also started to make "Elephant" Shelters in Kandahar Farm with 10 R.A.M.C.. This is the advanced dressing station. In the afternoon Lt Stronner reported with 11 men of his section	
	8th.		to 311th Bde R.F.A.. He worked for the Gunners on this day returning to camp in the evening.	

T2134. Wt. W708–776. 500000. 4/15. Sir J. C. & S.

Instructions regarding War Diaries and Intelligence Summaries are contained in F. S. Regs., Part II. and the Staff Manual respectively. Title pages will be prepared in manuscript.

WAR DIARY
or
INTELLIGENCE SUMMARY.
(Erase heading not required.)

Army Form C. 2118.

Place	Date	Hour	Summary of Events and Information	Remarks and references to Appendices
			Sept	
Neuve Eglise	8th incl.		2/Lt Prain reported to 47th Bde RFA. at 9 am at N. Midland Farm. while 2/Lt Elliott reported to 46th Bde RFA. for work. In the former case it meant a continuation of mule track to allow him to get his guns in position for a show on the 13th inst. The 46th wanted accomodation for personnel but had no stores so no work cd be done that day. No 1 Section & a few sappers of No 2 left behind were split up in small parties & carried on at Duck board track, mule track & Elephant shelter at Kandahar Farm. In addition 2/Lt Prain with 4 sappers was superintending construction of rifle range ~~at~~ outside Neuve Eglise. Work on track & duck board walk continued till	
"	16th		18th. Three Hundred infantry employed on the former in 3 shifts; during the last week an aeroplane dropped bombs on one party, but without causing casualties. Both of these useful sapper works. Hutting was begun on the 16th inst, a party of 100 Infantry being attached for labour. Work was begun under Lt Foster at SHANKHILL CAMP & under 2/Lt Stronner at Kortepyp. 2/Lt Elliott worked repairing camp for the Depot Battn near Div H.Q. He also began on a harness room for the 42nd Field Ambulance. Nissen huts are being erected in the 3 camps. The School in Neuve Eglise being repaired by Lt Foster – Retiling the roof & filling up the greatest	
	17th		holes with C.I. Lt Moore went on Home Leave 17th inst.	
	18th		Lt Foster started new job, handing over hutting works to 2/Lt Stronner. The D.D.O. (Lt Foster) is responsible for giving technical advice to units on the drainage of camps.	

WAR DIARY
or
INTELLIGENCE SUMMARY.
(Erase heading not required.)

Instructions regarding War Diaries and Intelligence Summaries are contained in F. S. Regs., Part II. and the Staff Manual respectively. Title pages will be prepared in manuscript.

Sept

Place	Date	Hour	Summary of Events and Information	Remarks and references to Appendices
Neuve Eglise	13th		no [illegible] are attached for work in connection with the hutting. The work continued satisfactorily & the weather remained fine. One section of sappers with infantry working party can erect 2 Nissen huts per day. It is essential that the preliminary work be most carefully done, levelling, squaring etc. There is always difficulty about these posts, the number of spares, bolts etc. should be considerably increased. W. Moore returned from leave 29/9/17	
"	30th		By 30th 56 huts have been erected at the following camps	
			24 at SHANKHILL, 11 at KORTEPYP 8 at [illegible] 9 at PENTANCE CAMP	
			1 at 41st Bde Transport lines, 2 at 42nd Bde Transport lines, 1 at [illegible]	
			In addition 1 cookhouse, 2 latrines have been made & trench board tracks laid in SHANKHILL. ~~two~~ Also 1 cookhouse has been made, orderly room rebuilt, extension to offrs mess made at DEPOT BN. Further for the 42nd Fd. Amb. a harness room, forage room, & smithy was made and repairs to horse standings carried out and for the 43rd Fd. Amb. a forage room was built and farriers room fitted with lockers.	

Instructions regarding War Diaries and Intelligence Summaries are contained in F. S. Regs., Part II. and the Staff Manual respectively. Title pages will be prepared in manuscript.

WAR DIARY
or
INTELLIGENCE SUMMARY.
(Erase heading not required.)

Army Form C. 2118.

Sept.

Place	Date	Hour	Summary of Events and Information	Remarks and references to Appendices
NEUVE EGLISE.			Satisfactory progress was made on the MULE TRACK to MIDDLE FARM, from 28/T5 b 60.85 –	
			From 28/T5 b 60 85 to BIRTHDAY RD old existing mud track was repaired, ditched, and fascined in the worst places –	
			From BIRTHDAY RD to MIDDLE FM C.R.E. decided to make a planked road. This portion was an unbroken succession of large shell craters mostly full of water – The formation of 1200x of this road was made up and 250x planked including 2 small bridges – Planking was delayed considerably by lack of material and all the work by the activity of hostile aeroplanes – On few occasions did shell fire stop the work, though on one afternoon and night 17 direct hits were obtained on the track –	
			E. [illegible] MAJOR R.E. (S.R.) O. C. 61st FIELD COY, R. E.	

1577 Wt. W10791/1773 500,000 1/15 D. D. & L. A.D.S.S./Forms/C. 2118.

Instructions regarding War Diaries and Intelligence Summaries are contained in F. S. Regs., Part II. and the Staff Manual respectively. Title pages will be prepared in manuscript.

WAR DIARY
or
INTELLIGENCE SUMMARY.
(Erase heading not required.)

October – 1917 –

Army Form C. 2118.

Vol 30

Place	Date	Hour	Summary of Events and Information	Remarks and references to Appendices
NEUVE EGLISE	1st–5th		No 1.2. & 3 Sections on hutting & repair of NEUVE EGLISE –	
			No 4 Section on Plank Road from BIRTHDAY ROAD to MIDDLE FARM –	
			Since 16th ult a total of 87 NISSEN huts were completed and 21 were in course of erection, a number of cookhouses were built, these latrines and ablution benches were fixed with brick, a clipping plate 100 ft was erected, stables for A.P.M's 26 horses & harness & forage rooms for same were nearly completed, several houses in NEUVE EGLISE repaired –	
	6th		Coy marched to WESTOUTRE AREA –	
			Lieut PRAIN and 25 men left behind as a handing-over party –	
	7th		Coy marched to DICKEBUSCH 28/H 34 1.1. – 11th Fd. Coy of 33rd Div. handed over.	
	8th		Work :- To complete planked road (PLUMER'S DRIVE SOUTH) from point in SANCTUARY WOOD to CLAPHAM JUNCTION to join up with PLUMER'S DRIVE NORTH –	
			Nos 1 & 2 Sections under 2 Lieut SKONNER worked in morning,	
			Nos 3 & 4 " " " ELTOFF went out in afternoon but unable to get near the work owing to shelling – Inf. officer said to-day was the 1st day's work possible for 4 days –	

Army Form C. 2118.

WAR DIARY
or
INTELLIGENCE SUMMARY.
(Erase heading not required.)

Instructions regarding War Diaries and Intelligence Summaries are contained in F. S. Regs., Part II. and the Staff Manual respectively. Title pages will be prepared in manuscript. October 1917.

Place	Date	Hour	Summary of Events and Information	Remarks and references to Appendices
	9th		C.R.E. ordered no work. General attack of French, Fifth, and part of Second Army —	
	10th		Nos 1 & 2 worked on PLUMER DRIVE SOUTH in morning under 2 Lt STRONNER. Quite a fair mornings work.	
			Nos 3 & 4 were prevented from reaching work by shelling.	
			Handed this work over to 59th Fd. Cy. R.E. 5th Div —	
			Took over work in the line from 11th Fd. Cy R.E. 33rd Div.	
	11th		Work in this sector was much disorganized by the recent attacking but all work taken over was the making of duckboard tracks — No. 3 Sect commenced work on a track starting from the MENIN ROAD and skirting INVERNESS COPSE by about 100 to 150 yds — No carrying party —	
			Nos 1, 2 & 4 Sects worked on G track which is to extend from Plank Road near DORMY HOUSE at 28 I 23 a 25.32 to PLUMER DRIVE SOUTH at 28 J. 13. c. 35. 60. No carrying party —	
	12th		Nos 3 & 4 on G track — Pioneers put on track round INVERNESS COPSE — Nos. 1 & 2 on providing accomodation for 1 Bn at BEDFORD HOUSE. Lieut PRAIN marked out track from PLUMER DRIVE SOUTH to INVERNESS COPSE —	

1577 Wt. W10791/1773 500,000 1/15 D. D. & L. A.D.S.S./Forms/C. 2118.

Instructions regarding War Diaries and Intelligence Summaries are contained in F. S. Regs., Part II. and the Staff Manual respectively. Title pages will be prepared in manuscript.

WAR DIARY
or
INTELLIGENCE SUMMARY.
(Erase heading not required.)

Army Form C. 2118.

October 1917.

Place	Date	Hour	Summary of Events and Information	Remarks and references to Appendices
DICKEBUSCHE	13th – 22nd		During this period 2 Sects worked on G Track and 2 Sections on providing accomodation at BEDFORD HOUSE. These 2 first named Sections with 50 Inf. laid some 1700x of single duck board track and some 750x of this was doubled. In all bad places this track was placed on piles – E Track was repaired daily by a small maintenance party – Other small works done by these 2 Sectns (i) making a waterproof visual signalling station at Bde Hqs. After completing this the Hun fired 6 shells at it & obtained a direct hit with 6th shot – Hence it had to be rebuilt – (ii) Cutting a slit in tower ~~[illegible]~~ at J14 d 9 4 (Eastern Edge of INVERNESS COPSE) in order to enable visual signalling communication to be carried on under cover from Support Bn – within 80x of the tower – and Bde Hqs. Three days work was done on this and 1'8" progress was made on the inside & 1' on the outside – So well was the reinforced concrete built – (iii) Erecting notice boards on duckboard track –	

1577 Wt. W10791/1773 500,000 1/15 D. D. & L. A.D.S.S./Forms/C. 2118.

Instructions regarding War Diaries and Intelligence Summaries are contained in F. S. Regs., Part II. and the Staff Manual respectively. Title pages will be prepared in manuscript.

WAR DIARY
or
INTELLIGENCE SUMMARY.
(Erase heading not required.)

Army Form C. 2118.

October 1917.

Place	Date	Hour	Summary of Events and Information	Remarks and references to Appendices
DICKEBUSCHE			Work on the G track was appreciably interfered with by hostile shelling and generally the whole sector was distinctly lively.	
			Work at BEDFORD HOUSE –	
			Six huts (36'x14') made of felt roof & sides, sandbag walls up to 3', were built for men. One hut of this type for officers.	
			Two NISSEN huts with C.I. lining were erected. The first was built complete, by 12 Sappers, except for ~~[struck out]~~ fixing piles, which were fixed previously, – in 2 3/4 hours, which is a record. The second was erected by the same number of men in 3 hours –	
			In addition incinerators, latrines, cookhouses etc were erected. Work was delayed by lack of material –	
	~~33~~ 23rd.		E & G tracks repaired – Work at BEDFORD HOUSE completed –	
			All work handed over to 39th Fd. Coy R.E. 5th Div. –	

Instructions regarding War Diaries and Intelligence Summaries are contained in F. S. Regs., Part II. and the Staff Manual respectively. Title pages will be prepared in manuscript.

WAR DIARY
or
INTELLIGENCE SUMMARY.
(Erase heading not required.)

Army Form C. 2118.

Place	Date	Hour	Summary of Events and Information October 1917	Remarks and references to Appendices
DICKEBUSCHE	24th		Division relieved to-night & withdrawn. R.E., Pioneers and 1 Bn (D.C.L.I.) remained in present camps & placed at disposal of C.E. X Corps.	
			Work allotted to 61st Fd Coy was to complete PLUMER'S DRIVE SOUTH up to MENIN ROAD in the vicinity of CLAPHAM JUNCTION.	
			1 Coy Pioneers, 2 Coys Infy to assist.	
	25th		Commenced work on PLUMER'S DRIVE. Work handicapped by the small carrying party as the 2 Coys allotted only were able to turn out 104 strong. Nevertheless 30x plank track were laid & there left 100x to do. 1 Coy Kings Pioneers worked on formation.	
	26th		No work done. General attack – not successful on X Corps Front.	
	27th		Nos 1, 2, & 3 Secs on Plank Road, 1 Coy Pioneers on formation, 3 Coys Infantry carrying. R.E. & Pioneers carried up slabs on the way up. 40 yds laid. Work limited by small carrying parties.	

Instructions regarding War Diaries and Intelligence Summaries are contained in F. S. Regs., Part II. and the Staff Manual respectively. Title pages will be prepared in manuscript.

WAR DIARY
or
INTELLIGENCE SUMMARY.
(Erase heading not required.)

Army Form C. 2118.

Place	Date	Hour	Summary of Events and Information	Remarks and references to Appendices
			October 1917.	
DICKEBUSCH	28th		Nos 1, 2 & 3 Sect went up but were caught by the barrage put up by the Hun in ~~retaliation~~ retaliation to our practice barrage – Thirteen casualties were caused & these probably could have been avoided if I had been warned of our practice barrage – These Sections spent all the morning carrying back their wounded to WOODCOTE HOUSE – the nearest dressing station. Some 5000 yds. – and hence no work was done – L Cpl. H. E. WARREN showed great gallantry in attending to the wounded under the heavy shell fire –	
			No 4 Sect. went up in the afternoon and laid 25 yds. This was all the material carried up by the 1 Coy King's, 1 Bn D.C.L.I (strength about 160) who were supposed to do three journeys –	
			Spr. J. W. HARKER did very well in dressing & carrying out a wounded gunner from his battery position, which all the other gunners had left owing to the shelling –	
	29th		Nos 1, 2 & 3 Sect laid 60 yds. – 2 Sections of 62 Fd. Coy R.E. were lent to me and expedited the foundation a very good piece of work –	

T2134. Wt. W708–776. 500000. 4/15. Sir J. C. & S.

Instructions regarding War Diaries and Intelligence Summaries are contained in F. S. Regs., Part II. and the Staff Manual respectively. Title pages will be prepared in manuscript.

WAR DIARY
or
INTELLIGENCE SUMMARY.
(Erase heading not required.)

Army Form C. 2118.

Place	Date	Hour	Summary of Events and Information — October - 1917 -	Remarks and references to Appendices
DICKEBUSCH	29th		1 Bn DCLI. carried up slabs but did not get the three stipulated journeys done - ~~1 Bn~~ 3 Cys Kings carried for 1 journey and 1 Cy for 3 journeys - 80 yds still remain to be done. This can quite easily be laid in 1 shift, if only the material can be got onto the site -	
	30th		No work - attack -	
	31st		Nos 2, 3 & 4 Sec. completed PLUMER'S DRIVE SOUTH to the MENIN RD - 102 yds of plank ~~road~~ were laid and 8 shells holes in the formation filled up - This 102 yards included 21 yards of track relaid over shell holes -	
			1 Bn Som L.I & 11th Kings carried up some 500 slabs which left some 30 over for repairs -	
			In the 5 days work on PLUMER'S DRIVE 257 yds of planking were laid. This is considerably above the average of previous Divisions on the same work. The work was done in a somewhat heavily shelled area and proved trying work to officers and men -	

[signature] Major 2.11.17
MAJOR R. E. (S. R.)
O. C. 61st FIELD COY, R. E.

WAR DIARY
or
INTELLIGENCE SUMMARY.
(*Erase heading not required.*)

Army Form C. 2118.

Instructions regarding War Diaries and Intelligence Summaries are contained in F. S. Regs., Part II. and the Staff Manual respectively. Title pages will be prepared in manuscript.

November — 1917.

61st Field Co

Vol 31

Place	Date	Hour	Summary of Events and Information	Remarks and references to Appendices
DICKEBUSCH	1st		A letter of appreciation received from Corps Commander on the work done by this Coy in completing PLUMER'S DRIVE — Copy attached — (marked A)	A —
	1st		Coy rested —	
	2nd		Received orders for work on hutting and making horse lines from C.R.E. X Corps Troops — Coy employed on camps work, building horse lines, drainage, advanced billets at BELLAGOOD FM.	
	3rd – 8th		Worked on erecting huts, completing existing horse lines for R.F.A. —	
	6th		Lieut. HADLEY reported for duty from the Base.	
	9th		Stood by in camp for orders as I had been warned the previous night to cease work for C.R.E. X Corps and that the R.E. & Pioneers had been transferred to Canadian Corps —	
	10th		Marched to VLAMERTINGE — Reported to C.R.E. 1st Canadian Division — M.O. arrived from C.R.E. to be attached —	
	11th		Lieuts MOORE & 2nd Lt HADLEY & 2 N.C.O.s proceeded to POTIZE to take over work from 2nd Canadian Field Coy. In morning I took over the work, viz Plank Road, from O.C.	

Instructions regarding War Diaries and Intelligence Summaries are contained in F. S. Regs., Part II. and the Staff Manual respectively. Title pages will be prepared in manuscript.

WAR DIARY
or
INTELLIGENCE ~~SUMMARY.~~
(Erase heading not required.)

Army Form C. 2118.

November 1917 –

Place	Date	Hour	Summary of Events and Information	Remarks and references to Appendices
VLAMERTINGE	11th		No 1 Sect. under 2nd Lieut. ELTOFF marched to CAESTRE for rail for LONGUENESSE where they remained until 22nd when they rejoined the Coy by lorry –	
	12th		Nos 2 & 3 Sect marched up to POTIZE to billets vacated by 2nd Canadian Fd. Coy.	
POTIZE	13th		No 4 Sect & HQ moved up to POTIZE – Transport took over lines of same Fd. Coy. Nos 2 & 3 Sect worked on the PANET Plank Road –	
	14th–17th		Worked on the Plank Road doubling and repairing it in the vicinity of KANSAS CROSS – This road being the most Easterly of all plank roads is heavily shelled and the work of even repairing the shell holes is heavy – On the 14th 2 motor lorries were hit and caught fire, 3 G.S. wagons, 3 pontoon wagons, guns limbers, and several pack animals were also hit – An ammn dump at the edge of the road exploded & made a crater about 20x across – a diversion was made round the spot –	
		~~17th~~	~~Lieut – attended a reconnaissance of the SEINE – GRAVENSTAFEL Rd for C.R.S.~~	

Army Form C. 2118.

Instructions regarding War Diaries and Intelligence Summaries are contained in F. S. Regs., Part II. and the Staff Manual respectively. Title pages will be prepared in manuscript.

WAR DIARY
or
~~INTELLIGENCE SUMMARY.~~
(Erase heading not required.)

November 1917.

Place	Date	Hour	Summary of Events and Information	Remarks and references to Appendices
POTIZE	17th–18th		Took over work on KANSAS CROSS – SEINE 60 cm. Tramway from the 4th Canadian A.T. Coy.	
			On these 2 days various breaks from shell fire were repaired and a few hundred yards of planks were laid between the rails as a foothold for men pushing the trucks –	
	18th		Handed this work over to the 201st Fd. Coy. R.E.	
	19th–23rd		Worked on PANET Road at the head (Regina Cross) – the 62nd Coy took the early morning shift and 61st from noon to 6 p.m. –	
			All the material for this work had to be pushed some 1500x on tramway and owing to congestion on the tramway and breakages and lack of trucks it was extremely difficult to get the material up – Work was continually being hampered by shell fire, Lt HADLEY being wounded on 21st & Lt. PRAIN on the 22nd – An average of 35x per day was laid – Working Parties 125 Inf –	
	24th		Worked on a spur running North from PANET ROAD (at D15a07), 85x laid –	
			Working Party – 186. 5th K.S.L.I. Very quiet morning –	

A6945 Wt. W11422/M1160 350,000 12/16 D. D. & L. Forms/C./2118/14.

Confidential

CE VIII Corps No 425
14th Divn No G.S. 1189
CRE 14th Divn No C1427

G. O. C.

14th Divn

My Chief Engineer has brought to my notice the excellent work done by the Royal Engineers, the Pioneer Battalion, the 5th K.S.L.I. and the 9th K.R.R.C. of your Division in constructing and maintaining forward tactical roads during the time these units were working under his direction while your Division was at rest.

Only the urgent necessity of the situation compelled me to keep these units at work during this period.

Please convey to your C.R.E. Lt Col COLLINS, to Lt Col. BINGHAM commanding the 11th Kings (Liverpool) Regt to Lt Col SMITH commanding 5th K.S.L.I., to Lt Col. HOWARD BURY commanding the 9th K.R.R.C. and to all ranks under their commands my appreciation of, and thanks for the excellent work they performed under difficult circumstances

(sd) AYLMER HUNTER WESTON
Lt Gen
Commanding VIII Corps

C.R.E.

The G.O.C. 14th Divn has much pleasure in forwarding the above letter for your information

(Sd) ——— Lt Col
Gen Staff
14th (Light) Divn

O.C.
61st Field Coy R.E.

I have much pleasure in forwarding a copy of the attached letter, and at the same time wish to thank Major E.E.V TEMPERLEY, O.C. 61st Field Coy R.E., Major A.W.S. GIBSON O.C. 62nd Field Coy R.E. and Capt E.D. ALEXANDER Actg O.C. 89th Field Coy R.E. for their share in the above work

(Sd) W. S Collins Lt Col R.E.
C.R.E. 14th (Light) Divn

10.12.17

Instructions regarding War Diaries and Intelligence Summaries are contained in F. S. Regs., Part II. and the Staff Manual respectively. Title pages will be prepared in manuscript.

WAR DIARY
or
INTELLIGENCE SUMMARY.

December 1917 (*Erase heading not required.*)

61 Fd Coy R.E.

Vol 32

Army Form C. 2118.

Place	Date	Hour	Summary of Events and Information	Remarks and references to Appendices
POTIZE	1st		Worked on Spur North of PANET ROAD with 110 Inf. — 40 yds laid —	
	2nd		Handed over work to 15th Coy R.E. — Billets to 40th Div — Took over work from 2nd Fd Coy R.E.	
			This work consisted of laying but not maintaining a single trench board track from BELLEVUE to MOSSELMARKT — PASSCHENDALE Road — The result of no maintenance party working on this trench board track (No 5 Track) was that it was entirely useless as a track as east of BELLEVUE on an average not more than 6 continuous boards were intact — The trench boards lying around serve as a guide for the Infantry but nothing more —	
YPRES	3rd		Took over billets in YPRES from 15th Fd Coy R.E. — All the Coy accomodated well in cellars — Commenced work on No 5 track maintenance —	
	4th–14th		Worked on No 5 Track up to 10th and No 6 trench board track up to 14th — During this period 1411 trench boards were carried up & laid generally on piles and mostly in repairs —	

A6945 Wt. W11422/M1160 350,000 12/16 D. D. & L. Forms/C.2118/14.

Army Form C. 2118.

WAR DIARY
or
INTELLIGENCE SUMMARY.
(Erase heading not required.)

Instructions regarding War Diaries and Intelligence Summaries are contained in F. S. Regs., Part II. and the Staff Manual respectively. Title pages will be prepared in manuscript.

December 1917.

Place	Date	Hour	Summary of Events and Information	Remarks and references to Appendices
YPRES.	4th-14th		Further 1300 yards of single Apron Wire Fence was erected on the ABRAHAM - GRAVENSTAFEL Ridge - In addition certain small jobs were done for the Brigade in the line such as strengthening dugouts etc -	
			All the work in the forward area was carried out just after daybreak as it was found that as a rule up to 9.30 a.m or 10.30 a.m. was the quietest time of the day -	
	15th-25th		Work was handed over to and taken over from 80th Fd. Coy. R.E. During this period Pack trains were built, Shelters for Gunners, NISSEN Huts erected at ENGLISH CAMP and CALIFORNIA CAMP, Cut & cover shelters erected for the ½ Bn in occupation at SPREE FARM -	
	26th		Exchanged billets with 15th Fd. Coy. R.E. at farms between WATOU & POPERINGHE 27 L.14 b 0.4. - Transport marched - Sappers moved by lorries -	
	27th-30th		Rested and did a little drill - very cold and not very good billets -	
			Xmas dinner of men was held on 30th -	

A6945 Wt. W11422/M1160 350,000 12/16 D. D. & L. Forms/C./2118/14.

Army Form C. 2118.

WAR DIARY
or
INTELLIGENCE SUMMARY.
(*Erase heading not required.*)

Instructions regarding War Diaries and Intelligence Summaries are contained in F. S. Regs., Part II. and the Staff Manual respectively. Title pages will be prepared in manuscript.

December 1917.

Place	Date	Hour	Summary of Events and Information	Remarks and references to Appendices
	31st.		Marched to HARDIFORT en route to join the Division at ST. OMER –	
			Roads very bad with ice –	
			For work on PANET ROAD a letter of appreciation was	
			received from Corps Commander VIII Corps. Congratulations –	
			Personal :-	
	1st.		2nd Lieut A.W. PHILIPS – (T.) reported –	
	23rd.		2nd Lieut C. G. CATCHPOLE. (T.C.) " (Transferred from 216th Rd & RS)	

E. C. [illegible] (RE)
Major R.E.
O. C. 6th Rd. & RS
1.1.18.

A6945 Wt. W11422/M1160 350,000 12/16 D. D. & L. Forms/C./2118/14.

Instructions regarding War Diaries and Intelligence Summaries are contained in F. S. Regs., Part II. and the Staff Manual respectively. Title pages will be prepared in manuscript.

WAR DIARY
or
INTELLIGENCE SUMMARY.
(Erase heading not required.)

January 1918

Army Form C. 2118.

61 Fd Coy R.E.
Vol 33

Place	Date	Hour	Summary of Events and Information	Remarks and references to Appendices
	1st		Coy marched to ST-MARTIN-AU-LAERT —	
	2nd-3rd		Coy rested and drilled —	
	4th	2 am	Coy entrained at ST. OMER and detrained about midday at EDGE HILL — Weather was bitterly cold and roads like glass — After detraining, Coy marched to VAUX-SUR-SOMME —	
	22nd		Coy. marched out of VAUX-SUR-SOMME for VILLERS-AUX-ERABLES, after a rest period of 17 days, during which time a comprehensive training was undergone. The canalized SOMME gave the opportunity for pontooning & boat-drill. Demolition, rigging of spars, rifle drill & route marches were all done, with the result that the morale of the men as they swung along by the tow path to CORBIE was as high as it had ever been. During this period No3 section with, first Lt [illegible] & afterwards Lt [illegible] were detached to 5th ARMY school at TOUTENCOURT preparing an exhibition ground. They marched both ways with section transport.	
	23rd		Coy marched to ARVILLERS from VILLERS-AUX-ERABLES.	
	24th		The Coy. did its longest march since it has been in France, marching 26	

A6945 Wt. W11422/M1160 350,000 12/16 D. D. & L. Forms/C./2118/14.

Instructions regarding War Diaries and Intelligence Summaries are contained in F. S. Regs., Part II. and the Staff Manual respectively. Title pages will be prepared in manuscript.

WAR DIARY

or

INTELLIGENCE SUMMARY.

(Erase heading not required.)

Army Form C. 2118.

Place	Date	Hour	Summary of Events and Information — JANUARY	Remarks and references to Appendices
BEINES	24th		miles to BEINES, N.E. of Guiscard. No one fell out - Packs were not worn -	
JUSSY	25th	2pm	Coy. moved again to JUSSY where it arrived after dark.	
	26th		The Coy. took over from a French Fld Coy. at RAVINE-DES-SAULES situated midway between ESSIGNY-LE-GRAND & BENAY. No 3 section & the transport remained at JUSSY, the section to work for the C.R.E.	
Dugouts	27th		After reconnaissance, work was begun on the 28th completing dug-outs in	
Ravine des	28th		the strong point "CALVAIRE" & on the C.T. RUSSIE. Nos 2 & 4 sections ~~No~~ worked	
Saules	29th		on the dugouts. No 3 section worked at clearing out C.T. FRANCE.	
	30th		No 1 section with party of 150 Infantry began clearing out the support line between C.T.s SOMME & MARNE, as a preliminary to revetting posts in this line. 2/Lt Phillips is in charge of this work.	
	31st		2/Lt Stroomer with 50 Inf. began the same work as above but N of C.T. AISNE 2/Lt Phillips carried on with 100 Infantry.	
			Personal:- Lieut. E.D. MOORE left on 11.1.18 to take up appointment as 2nd in command of 218 Fd. Coy R.E. O.C. acted C.R.E. from 8.1.18 - 14.1.18. - Capt. S.M. HALLEY attached to French Field Coy 4.1.18 - 14.1.18	
New Year Honours:-			MAJOR E.E.V. TEMPERLEY R.E.(S.R.) M.C. LT E.D. MOORE - SGT. A. SHIPTON. No 41719 } "Mention" CPL. F. HILLMAN No 40148 }	

E.E.V. Temperley Major R.E.(S.R.)

A6945 Wt. W11422/M1160 350,000 12/16 D. D. & L. Forms/C./2118/14.

61 Fd Coy R.E.
Vol 34

Instructions regarding War Diaries and Intelligence Summaries are contained in F. S. Regs., Part II. and the Staff Manual respectively. Title pages will be prepared in manuscript.

Army Form C. 2118.

WAR DIARY
or
INTELLIGENCE SUMMARY.
(*Erase heading not required.*)

Place	Date	Hour	FEBRUARY Summary of Events and Information	Remarks and references to Appendices
RAVINE DES	1st		No 3 section remained at CLASTRES working under Lt Catchpole for the CRE until the	
SAULES			13th inst when the section was relieved by Lt Phillips & No 1 section. Lt Catchpole	
situated			however came up to work in the line on the 8th inst.	
between			The programme of work for the 3 sections in the line was the completion of dugouts	
ESSIGNY-LE-			in CALVAIRE T, RUSSIE T, & clearing out, fire-stepping & revetting certain	
GRAND & BENAY			portions of MAES & PECHINE trenches, wh. forms (the one trench is a	
about 5			continuation of the other) the support line. But it is in reality the line of	
miles from			resistance, the regular front line being held by a series of posts only at	
ST QUENTIN			the junctions of the C.T.s.	
	5th		Lt Stromner with No 2 section detached for work on Corps Line (a second position	
			begun by the French) & position resting on ESSIGNY-LE-GRAND. The	
			general trace of the line pretty well coincides with the work begun by	
			the French. The section of trench proposed by corps is the most	
			sensible I have seen, for work intended to stand without revetment.	
			The section is as shewn in the margin. It was an object lesson to the	For section
			infantry & I have noticed since a marked improvement in trench	of Trenches see P. 4.

A6945 Wt. W11422/M1160 350,000 12/16 D. D. & L. Forms/C./2118/14.

Instructions regarding War Diaries and Intelligence Summaries are contained in F. S. Regs., Part II. and the Staff Manual respectively. Title pages will be prepared in manuscript.

WAR DIARY
or
INTELLIGENCE SUMMARY.
(Erase heading not required.)

Army Form C. 2118.

Place	Date	Hour	FEBRUARY CONT. Summary of Events and Information	Remarks and references to Appendices
[illegible] 5			making in the line, a better slope to the sides, a good berm etc.	
miles from			Work on dug-outs, MAES & PECHINE TRS was carried on & both completed	
St QUENTIN	8th		the former about the 8th the latter about the 15th	
	12th		The construction of strong points around URVILLERS takes precedence of	
			other work in forward zone. From this date Lt Catchpole with No 3 Section began wiring	
	13th		LOUVOIS W. The garrison provided 1 N.C.O. & 9 men who worked under a	
			sapper NCO & sappers. A double double apron fence was the type of wiring	
			selected because of its invisibility.	
			Wiring was also begun on "CALVAIRE" strong point & a few days	
			later on MADELON. In the latter work a tunnel under the road	
			has to be enlarged, strutted & sheeted as a dug-out, of which 2 entrances	
			had been finished to be made.	
			The works Coy. the formation of which has been debated for some time	
			came into being. A platoon of the 8th KRR & another of the 7th RB are	
			attached to their Coy. from the 13th. Another platoon of the 8th RB	
			were attached on the . This gives the Fd. Coy. a permanent	

Instructions regarding War Diaries and Intelligence Summaries are contained in F. S. Regs., Part II. and the Staff Manual respectively. Title pages will be prepared in manuscript.

WAR DIARY
or
INTELLIGENCE SUMMARY.
(Erase heading not required.)

Army Form C. 2118.

Place	Date	Hour	FEBRUARY CONT. Summary of Events and Information	Remarks and references to Appendices
About 5 miles from St. Quentin			working party of 100. The arrangement works well, the men & officers are interested in the work. They are attached for a period of a month except in the case of the first relief, wh. is arranged to prevent more than 1 platoon being relieved in any week.	
	13th		[illegible] Working parties began work on a strong point round at battalion HQ.	
			Lt. Spencer with No 2 section (wh. was returned to the Coy on the 18th) carried on with work in MAES Tr. & AISNE C.T., in the former completion of dug out for Coy. H.Q., & revetting of firebays & in the latter sheeting the tunnel where the C.T. goes under the road.	
			In addition to these works, 2 O.P.s were made for 46th Bde R.F.A., consisting of a vertical shaft with an iron cupola on the top, 2 cut & cover shelters were constructed in 2 of the strong points & 6–10	
	~~th~~		sappers were engaged on Gas proof curtains.	
	25th		Lt. Jones began a new strong point South of ORVILLERS	

A6945 Wt. W11422/M1160 350,000 12/16 D. D. & L. Forms/C./2118/14.

Army Form C. 2118.

Instructions regarding War Diaries and Intelligence Summaries are contained in F. S. Regs., Part II. and the Staff Manual respectively. Title pages will be prepared in manuscript.

WAR DIARY
or
INTELLIGENCE SUMMARY.
(Erase heading not required.)

Place	Date	Hour	FEBRUARY CONT. Summary of Events and Information	Remarks and references to Appendices
Stables from St Quentin	28th		The 6 strong points etc. from the defences of URVILLERS are all well advanced. Louvois & RE Battn HQ & VERDUN are almost complete.	
			Personnel	
			O.C. leave UK 4th–24th Feb.	Leave
			No 40148 Cpl F Hillman was awarded the BELGIAN CROIX DE GUERRE	Honours

E. C. [signature]
MAJOR R.E. (S.R.)
O.C. 61st FIELD COY. R.E.

A6945 Wt. W11422/M1160 350,000 12/16 D. D. & L. Forms/C./2118/14.

14th Divisional Engineers

61st FIELD COMPANY R. E.

MARCH 1918

14

61 Fd Coy R.E.

Vol 35

Army Form C. 2118.

Instructions regarding War Diaries and Intelligence Summaries are contained in F. S. Regs., Part II. and the Staff Manual respectively. Title pages will be prepared in manuscript.

WAR DIARY
or
INTELLIGENCE ~~SUMMARY~~.
(Erase heading not required.)

March 1918 –

Place	Date	Hour	Summary of Events and Information	Remarks and references to Appendices
RAVINE DES SAULES 1 Km West of BENAY.	1st–20th		During this period the Coy was employed very fully on following works.	
			Works in Forward Area:–	
			(i) 5 strong points:– each of these was wired with a double belt of double apron fence, firebays were ~~prepared~~ built, trench stops provided.	
			(ii) Gas curtains:– All dugouts in forward area were provided with well made double gas curtains. This work proved very slow owing to lack of an ample supply of material.	
			(iii) Dugouts:– In MADELON S.P. the dugout in course of construction was practically completed. In RUSSIA C.T. the 2 existing slopes were joined up by a pilot tunnel. A tunnel under the road at MADELON ~~S.P.~~ S.P. was completed. Dugout in the support line started and [illegible].	
			(iv) O.P.S. O.P. for D/46 Bde R.F.A. completed. H15c93 and a second provided with splinter proof cover.	
			Battle Area:–	
			One section was employed on this with working parties varying from one to two battalions and 1½ Coys of 11th Kings Pioneers.	

A6945 Wt. W11422/M1160 350,000 12/16 D. D. & L. Forms/C./2118/14.

Instructions regarding War Diaries and Intelligence Summaries are contained in F. S. Regs., Part II. and the Staff Manual respectively. Title pages will be prepared in manuscript.

WAR DIARY
or
~~INTELLIGENCE~~ SUMMARY.
(Erase heading not required.)

Army Form C. 2118.

March 1918.

Place	Date	Hour	Summary of Events and Information	Remarks and references to Appendices
RAVINE DES SAULES			The battle zone was arranged in depth of 4 lines of continuous trenches dug out to depth in certain places with some 10 defended localities to hold on an average of 1½ platoons with all round defence. All these strong points except one were protected by a double belt of double apron fence -	
	20th		Put all available men on to completing gas curtains in forward area and battle zone. This entailed 8 to 10 hours work. After which 1 Tunnelling section sent to put wire out all round the unwired S.P. in Battle Zone - This was completed -	
			At 3.20 p.m. the message was received "Battle Zone take precautionary action". I had expected this message as information had been received from prisoners that attack was likely to take place in the early morning of the 21st -	
			I had orders from C.R.E. to recall all ranks to Hqrs on receipt of this message & be ready to move at 15 mins notice. Nevertheless I considered it advisable for men to complete gas curtains before returning -	

A6945 Wt. W11422/M1160 350,000 12/16 D. D. & L. Forms/C./2118/14.

Instructions regarding War Diaries and Intelligence Summaries are contained in F. S. Regs., Part II. and the Staff Manual respectively. Title pages will be prepared in manuscript.

WAR DIARY
or
INTELLIGENCE SUMMARY.
(Erase heading not required.)

Army Form C. 2118.

March 1918.

Place	Date	Hour	Summary of Events and Information	Remarks and references to Appendices
RAVINE DES SAULES.	20th.		The work in the forward area was carried out in conjunction with the Bn holding the line and assisted by the Works Coy, which consisted of a platoon with 1 off from each Bn in the Bde – although these platoons were relieved by the Bns once a month the system of the Works Coy proved very satisfactory –	
	21st.		Woken up at 4.20 a.m. by a violent bombardment commencing and having ordered the Coy to "stand to" – ~~[illegible]~~ No telephonic communication was possible with 41st Inf Bde but at 7.10 a.m. I found out from 42 Inf Bde that the message "Infantry occupy Battle Zone" had been sent out at in the night – Hence I ordered 2 Lieut KING in charge of a Works Platoon accomodated at the RAVINE DES SAULES to proceed to LA SABLIERE in accordance with previous orders issued by the Bde – I do not think he ever reached LA SABLIERE as I saw him ~~[illegible]~~ in the afternoon with 8th RB on near side of ESSIGNY and very few of the garrison of LA SABLIERE returned	
			In the vicinity of the dugouts bombardment was severe but no guns	

A6945 Wt. W11422/M1160 350,000 12/16 D. D. & L. Forms/C./2118/14.

4

Instructions regarding War Diaries and Intelligence Summaries are contained in F. S. Regs., Part II. and the Staff Manual respectively. Title pages will be prepared in manuscript.

WAR DIARY
or
~~INTELLIGENCE SUMMARY.~~
(Erase heading not required.)

Army Form C. 2118.

Place	Date	Hour	March 1918 – Summary of Events and Information	Remarks and references to Appendices
RAVINE DES	21st		also the calibre of 150 mm seemed to be used – At about 8 a.m.	
SAULES.			I sent 2 Lieut PHILIPS and No 1 Sect. to report to 41st Bde. H.qrs in accordance	
			with previous orders – On the appearance of the enemy in the	
			vicinity of Bde H.qrs about noon this section did a	
			good deal of fighting as may be grasped from the fact that	
			the majority of the Sappers fired off anything from 35 to 50	
			rounds of ammunition which was all they had in their possession. – They and a	
			few Engrs and some of Bde Hq staff were the entire force	
			for a period guarding Bde H.qrs until 8th R.B. came up on	
			the right and some R.I.R.s of the 36th Div on the left – This	
			Section was withdrawn shortly after dusk and	
			proceeded to FLAVY to join the Coy.	
			Up to about 11.30 a.m a very heavy ground mist prevailed	
			generally so thick that it was impossible to see 30 yards	
			ahead – at 12.10 p.m. an orderly from 42nd Bde H.qrs arrived	
			saying that the Germans had broken through and the everyone was	

A6945 Wt. W11422/M1160 350,000 12/16 D. D. & L. Forms/C./2118/14.

5/

Instructions regarding War Diaries and Intelligence Summaries are contained in F. S. Regs., Part II. and the Staff Manual respectively. Title pages will be prepared in manuscript.

WAR DIARY
or
~~INTELLIGENCE SUMMARY.~~
(*Erase heading not required.*)

Army Form C. 2118.

Place	Date	Hour	Summary of Events and Information	Remarks and references to Appendices
			March 1918.	
	21st		was retiring – Therefore I fell in the Coy outside the dugouts in fighting order – This meant leaving packs behind – On falling in outside the dugouts I found numerous stragglers falling back, these were collected with the help of 2 sections of 62nd Fd. Coy R.E. and 1 Wales Platoon attached to 62 Fd. Coy R.E. who had reported to me about 10 a.m. by order of their O.C. for what reason I do not know – The entire force then manned the reserve line of the Battle Zone defences – I chose this line as it was close to the dugouts and I considered it advisable to hold on to some line as quickly as possible as I knew nothing of the situation – I got into touch with 8th R.B. on my left who were holding the Reserve Line of the Battle Zone and the trench in front of it called FANNY & FREDDY. On the right I got into touch with the 43rd Inf. Bde. about 1 Km. South of BENAY where the front line of the Bde lay about 2.30 p.m. The position of 42 Inf. Bde was obscure but generally followed the continuation of FANNY & FREDDY in the 42 Bde Area –	

A6945 Wt. W11422/M1160 350,000 12/16 D. D. & L. Forms/C./2118/14.

6

Instructions regarding War Diaries and Intelligence Summaries are contained in F. S. Regs., Part II. and the Staff Manual respectively. Title pages will be prepared in manuscript.

WAR DIARY
or
INTELLIGENCE SUMMARY.
(Erase heading not required.)

Army Form C. 2118.

Place	Date	Hour	Summary of Events and Information	Remarks and references to Appendices
			March 1918.	
	21st	2.30 p.m.	No attack followed by Germans – Situation quiet except for shelling by 77mm guns and long range M.G. fire – At dusk sent to 41st Bde Hqs for orders and found that orders were expected ordering a general retirement to the JUSSY line. Received orders to withdraw to FLAVY at about 10 p.m. and withdrew whole force to R.S. transport lines at FLAVY. Slept the night at a Lewis camp near DETROIT BLEU.	
	22nd		Found C.R.E.'s Hqs at DETROIT BLEU and moved Coy to the transport lines at DETROIT D'ANNOIS – The majority of No 1 Sec. & 2 Lieut PHILLIPS turned up at transport camp at ~~[illegible]~~ early in the morning – Returned 62 Fd Coy R.E. sections to their Coy – At about 1 p.m. I found that field guns were in position and in action in rear of DETROIT D'ANNOIS and so in conjunction with O.C. 62 Fd Coy R.E. I decided to move Coy less No 2 Sec back to a point 1 Km South of CUGNY. This was done about 2 p.m. – By C.R.E.'s order I sent 2 Lieut STRONNER to report to B.G.C. 41 Inf Bde at FLAVY to say that 2 sections R.E. were at his disposal if required – B.G.C. 41 replied he did not require these sections as he was being relieved by 42 Inf Bde –	

A6945 Wt. W11422/M1160 350,000 12/16 D. D. & L. Forms/C./2118/14.

7

Instructions regarding War Diaries and Intelligence Summaries are contained in F. S. Regs., Part II. and the Staff Manual respectively. Title pages will be prepared in manuscript.

WAR DIARY
or
~~INTELLIGENCE SUMMARY.~~
(Erase heading not required.)

Army Form C. 2118.

Place	Date	Hour	Summary of Events and Information	Remarks and references to Appendices
1 KM. SOUTH OF CUGNY	22nd		No. 4 Section under 2 Lieut T. G. MAKEIG – JONES returned from JUSSY. This Section was employed before the 21st under the C.R.E. on rear line work such as baths etc and at the commencement of the battle was at CLASTRES. This section went to JUSSY to help Capt HALLET to load up transport and in the night of 21st–22nd was used by C.R.E. to assist 62nd Fd. Coy R.E. to destroy the bridges on the canal at JUSSY – Some 5 bridges were destroyed by the Sect. in addition to the assistance they gave to 62nd Fd. Coy. R.E. – In the morning of 22nd they were kept in reserve to the 5th LANCERS but being no longer required they withdrew about 3 p.m.	
		8 p.m.	Orders received from C.R.E. for all transport less tool carts to move to BEINES – Completed by 11.20 p.m.	
	23rd		Recalled No 2 Sect from old billet at DETROIT D'ANNOIS as they were not required by 41st Inf. Bde in the line. In accordance with C.R.E.'s orders I moved Coy back to BEAUMONT to await further orders. Tool carts were sent to GUIVRY under 2 Lieut JONES.	

A6945 Wt. W11422/M1160 350,000 12/16 D. D. & L. Forms/C./2118/14.

8

Instructions regarding War Diaries and Intelligence Summaries are contained in F. S. Regs., Part II. and the Staff Manual respectively. Title pages will be prepared in manuscript.

WAR DIARY
or
INTELLIGENCE SUMMARY.
(Erase heading not required.)

Army Form C. 2118.

Place	Date	Hour	Summary of Events and Information	Remarks and references to Appendices
	23rd	noon.	Coy set out with 62nd Fd. Coy R.E. under my orders to form a defensive flank from MONTALIMONT FM (Sheet 66D) Q 23 d. 3. 6. to road 1 KM west of CUGNY at R 19 a 5 5. I divided the sector up into 2 for position and ~~with~~ put 62nd Fd Coy R.E. on the right and 61st Fd. Coy R.E. on the left. Force in position by 1.30 p.m. About 3.30 p.m. a number of stragglers chiefly of 36th Divn commenced retiring from the direction of BROUCHY and continued coming back till about 5.30 pm by which time ~~until~~ some 500 or 600 were collected. These were rallied and placed in position from Q 24 d to ~~Q2~~ road about Q 22 central and placed under orders of a colonel who had established his H.qrs at MONTALIMONT FARM – About 2.30 p.m. ~~about~~ 70 of the 11th Kings, under Maj JOHNSON and 2 sections 89th Fd Coy R.E. arrived at R 25 a 3. 8 to strengthen the defensive flank already under orders of C.R.E. – The Kings took up a position stretching from the right of 62nd Fd Coy R.E. to road ~~about~~ at R 20 a 6.7. and they were in touch with a D.C.L.I. Bn of 20th (?) Divn on their right –	

A6945 Wt. W11422/M1160 350,000 12/16 D. D. & L. Forms/C./2118/14.

Instructions regarding War Diaries and Intelligence Summaries are contained in F. S. Regs., Part II. and the Staff Manual respectively. Title pages will be prepared in manuscript.

9

WAR DIARY
or
INTELLIGENCE SUMMARY.
(Erase heading not required.)

Army Form C. 2118.

Place	Date	Hour	Summary of Events and Information	Remarks and references to Appendices
			March 1918.	
	23rd		About 4.30 p.m. after very heavy M.G. fire, shouting and light blowing a number of men were seen retiring over the crest of the hill at R26 but these were rallied and held on to the reverse slope –	
			At ~~5.30 pm~~ 6 p.m I conferred with O.C. 62nd Fd. Coy R.E. & O.C. 89th Fd. Coy R.E. who had arrived about 3.30 p.m to take command of ~~the~~ his Coy and explained the situation to them which was (i) that our troops were dug in ~~at~~ R7b central and R8d central and on that sector no attack had developed (ii) that a strong force of 36th Div were holding the left flank at R.5 in front of MONTALIMONT FARM & (iii) that it appeared as though our front line position on the CUGNY heights in R26 had been apparently pierced as troops had been falling back –	
			My orders from C.R.E. were to hold the defensive flank to cover the approach of the French who were to take up a line near BROUCHY probably by 4.30 p.m – I considered that the danger was likely not from the North but from a point about 1000x South of CUGNY.	
			Therefore I considered that the 3 Field Coys R.E. consisted of detachment of	

A6945 Wt. W11422/M1160 350,000 12/16 D. D. & L. Forms/C./2118/14.

10.

Instructions regarding War Diaries and Intelligence Summaries are contained in F. S. Regs., Part II. and the Staff Manual respectively. Title pages will be prepared in manuscript.

WAR DIARY
or
INTELLIGENCE SUMMARY.
(Erase heading not required.)

Army Form C. 2118.

Place	Date	Hour	Summary of Events and Information	Remarks and references to Appendices
			March 1918.	
			11th Kings, should fall back and form a strong point of BEAULIEU (Q 36) so as to (i) form a rallying point for the position in front (ii) to cover the French if they came up and of whom no signs had yet been seen – Both O.C. Corps agreed and MAJOR JOHNSON of the 11th Kings was appointed – Sectors round the village of BEAULIEU were allotted to each unit –	
BEAULIEU	23rd		I arrived at BEAULIEU about 7.30 p.m. and found many stragglers returning from the front line – These I collected and having reorganised them with the Sappers ordered them to dig in and come under my orders –	
			about 10 p.m. the 1st R.I.R. (36th Div.?) ~~[illegible]~~ about 130 strong, arrived from the front in an exhausted state. I explained the situation to the C.O. and placed myself and my stragglers under his orders – He put his Bn on the Northern face of the village thus filling a gap between left of 61st [illegible] and right of 62nd [illegible] ~~[illegible] our all round system of defence~~	

A6945 Wt. W1422/M1160 350,000 12/16 D. D. & L. Forms/C./2118/14.

11

WAR DIARY
or
INTELLIGENCE SUMMARY.
(Erase heading not required.)

Army Form C. 2118.

Instructions regarding War Diaries and Intelligence Summaries are contained in F. S. Regs., Part II. and the Staff Manual respectively. Title pages will be prepared in manuscript.

Place	Date	Hour	Summary of Events and Information	Remarks and references to Appendices
			March 1918.	
BEAULIEU	23rd		On arrival at BEAULIEU a few French posts and M.G.s were holding a line from R 31 b 2.4, R 31 a 1.7 to Q 36 a 9.7.	
			The French believed similar small posts were again on their flanks.	
			During the night the Coy with help of stragglers dug themselves in from R 31 a 1.7 round the S.W. face of village to about Q 36 d 7.4. The 62 Fd. Coy R.E. had lined a hedge from road at Q 36 d 2.8 to Q 36 b 2.3 and the 89 Fd. Coy R.E. had formed a defensive flank on the north of the village.	
			The 11th King's dug themselves in from Q 36 b 1.5 to Q 36 a 9.7. Thus by dawn defence of the village had been provided for in the shape of a horse shoe. Uneventful night.	
	24th		The Bn of R.I.R. left about 6 a.m. to take up a new position in Q 30 b by orders of its own Brigade.	
			The 62 Fd. Coy R.E. and 89 Fd. Coy R.E. departed under orders from Major ORMISTON R.E. between 5.30 a.m. and 6 a.m.	

A6945 Wt. W11422/M1160 350,000 12/16 D. D. & L. Forms/C./2118/14.

12

Instructions regarding War Diaries and Intelligence Summaries are contained in F. S. Regs., Part II. and the Staff Manual respectively. Title pages will be prepared in manuscript.

WAR DIARY
or
INTELLIGENCE SUMMARY.
(Erase heading not required.)

Army Form C. 2118.

Place	Date	Hour	Summary of Events and Information	Remarks and references to Appendices
			March 1918	
BEAULIEU	24th		With cordial co-operation of Major JOHNSON we rearranged the troops to still maintain our horse shoe defence scheme and arranged to get trenches well dug – This was done and defences soon reached a satisfactory stage – At 11.30 received very definite orders from the 14th Div to retire immediately with all details to Farm 1 mile. South of VILLESELVE but as the approach of German cavalry in force on the Forge had been reported to me I considered that we should hold BEAULIEU until attack had been dealt with – The attack by cavalry did not materialize and after nothing beyond cavalry patrols were seen and here at 12 noon I withdrew 61st Fd Coy R.E. and the stragglers, who by this time consisted of 4 Off. 100 O.R. of 13th Gloucesters 3 Off 31 O.R. of 41st Inf Bde, 3 Off 27 O.R. of 42nd Inf Bde, 24 O.R. of 43rd Inf Bde, 30 O.R. of 20th & 36th D.W., 30 O.R. of Div. unknown, a total of 10 Off. 242 O.R., and gave the necessary orders to the 11th Kings – As soon as the party had left the village the enemy shelled the village very heavily and followed up the retirement up to the Farm with heavy shelling which was always short and caused no casualties –	

A6945 Wt. W11422/M1160 350,000 12/16 D. D. & L. Forms/C./2118/14.

13.

Instructions regarding War Diaries and Intelligence Summaries are contained in F. S. Regs., Part II. and the Staff Manual respectively. Title pages will be prepared in manuscript.

WAR DIARY
or
~~INTELLIGENCE SUMMARY.~~
(Erase heading not required.)

Army Form C. 2118.

Place	Date	Hour	Summary of Events and Information	Remarks and references to Appendices
			March 1918.	
BEINES.	24th	12.50pm	Arrived at FARM 1KM S. of ~~to~~ VILLESELVE where I received orders from	Ref.
			14th Div to join 41st Inf. Bde at BEINES and to return all stragglers to	Sheet 66D
			their various Bdes ~~and~~ and Divisions whose points of concentration were	ST. QUENTIN 18.
			given – As information had been received that enemy had broken through	
			on our right and left 41st Inf Bde decided to form a hollow	
			square at W 9 a 5.6. – This was done ~~and~~ but about 3.30 pm. orders were	
BUCHOIRE			received from Div. to retire on BUCHOIRE where after an hours halt	
GUESNY			further orders were received to retire to CROISELLES. The enemy	
CROISELLES.			commenced shelling both 2 villages with 77 m.m. guns as we passed	
			through – Rested at CROISELLES from 6.30 p.m. to 10.30 p.m. during this time	
			Lt. MOORE and 20 men of 89th Fd. Coy R.E. joined up in a very exhausted	
BEAURAINS			condition – Marched to LA ~~ve~~ VIGNETTE – 1 KM. S.W. of SERMAIZE – where	Ref. Sheet
LA VIGNETTE	25th		we arrived about 1.30 a.m. At 8.30 a.m. I received orders from 41st Inf. Bde	70E
			to take up a position from G 29 d central to X roads G 28 b 0.8 with M.G. Bn on	AMIENS 17
			left and 8th R.B. on the right in order to cover the 42nd & 43 Inf Bdes,	
			who were holding the canal in front at HARDIVAL & BEAURAINS, if forced to retire –	

A6945 Wt. W11422/M1160 350,000 12/16 D. D. & L. Forms/C./2118/14.

14

Instructions regarding War Diaries and Intelligence Summaries are contained in F. S. Regs., Part II. and the Staff Manual respectively. Title pages will be prepared in manuscript.

WAR DIARY
or
~~INTELLIGENCE SUMMARY.~~
(Erase heading not required.)

Army Form C. 2118.

Place	Date	Hour	Summary of Events and Information	Remarks and references to Appendices
			March 1918.	
LAVIGNETTE	25th		42nd & 43rd Inf Bdes commenced retiring through the 41st Bde at about 6.30 p.m. and were clear by 7 p.m. and then whole line of 41st Inf Bde was withdrawn without fighting and without contact having been obtained with the enemy in accordance with orders issued by the 41st Bde at 6.40 p.m.	Ref Sheet 70E & AMIENS 17
DIVE LE FRANCE			Reformed up at DIVE LE FRANCE and moved to EVRICOURT	
EVRICOURT			where at orders were received from the Division to proceed to THIESCOURT.	
THIESCOURT.			Very cold night and all men quite exhausted – As far as I saw there were no troops holding the line between THIESCOURT and the enemy as the French had been straggling back all the afternoon – Nevertheless all had an excellent night and nothing untoward happened –	
	26th		In the absence of definite orders from the Division 41st 42nd & 43rd Inf Bdes moved off to wood 1½ West of THIESCOURT in order to escape any shelling of the village – about 10 a.m. orders were received to proceed to ÉCOUVILLON where we arrived about 1.30 p.m. & proceeded to reconnoitre a position to take up if ordered in N 17 & N 10.	

A6945 Wt. W11422/M1160 350,000 12/16 D. D. & L. Forms/C./2118/14.

15.

Instructions regarding War Diaries and Intelligence Summaries are contained in F. S. Regs., Part II. and the Staff Manual respectively. Title pages will be prepared in manuscript.

WAR DIARY
or
INTELLIGENCE SUMMARY.
(Erase heading not required.)

Army Form C. 2118.

Place	Date	Hour	Summary of Events and Information	Remarks and references to Appendices
			March 1918	
	26th		In the course of the afternoon French troops began to arrive and finally to our great relief we were told to go back to ELINCOURT as the French no longer required us.	Ref. Sheet 70E AMIENS 17.
ELINCOURT	27th		At 1.30pm marched to Farm 2 miles N.E. of ROUVILLERS where stayed the night with 8th R.B.	BEAUVAIS 21
ROUVILLERS	28th		About 9.30 am orders came from Bde ~~came~~ that ~~to take up a position in the neighbourhood of the FARM~~ that the Brigade would take up a position from the ESTREES ST DENIS – GOURNAY Road to GRANDVILLERS to support the 2nd Cavalry Division on our left as the situation was obscure and it was not definitely known what troops were in front of us. The Bn had a front of about 700x about ½ mile N of the FARM with 8th R.B. on the right and 14th Entrenching Bn on the left.	
		2.30pm	Orders were received to withdraw from position taken up and to be ready to move to billets in the vicinity of PONT ST. MAXENCE.	
		4.30pm	8th RB received orders to move off and Bde informed us that Divn would issue orders for my move to me direct.	

A6945 Wt. W11422/M1160 350,000 12/16 D. D. & L. Forms/C./2118/14.

16

Instructions regarding War Diaries and Intelligence Summaries are contained in F. S. Regs., Part II. and the Staff Manual respectively. Title pages will be prepared in manuscript.

WAR DIARY
or
INTELLIGENCE SUMMARY.
(Erase heading not required.)

Army Form C. 2118.

Place	Date	Hour	Summary of Events and Information	Remarks and references to Appendices
			March 1918	
ROUVILLERS	28th		Waited till 6 p.m. for orders from Division and then decided to move off without orders to BEAUREPAIRE, my destination, alone. I arrived at 11.30 p.m. after a march of 15 miles in pouring rain – Nevertheless at BEAUREPAIRE we picked up Capt HARLEY & all the Transport thus enabling each man to have a blanket and full rations – Coy exhausted –	Ref Sheet BEAUVAIS 21
BEAUREPAIRE	29th		Marched to NOGENT to embus with the Division & for the Transport to proceed with Div'l Transport by road – Busses not sufficient to take the R.E. & have billeted the night in NOGENT	
NOGENT	30th		Marched to BIZANCOURT after march in rain. Men all wet through & again –	
BIZANCOURT	31st		" " VELLENES	
			Considerations on the employment of R.E. during the battle –	
			Owing to the violence of the attack and the consequent heavy losses ~~my~~ incurred by the Division this Coy was employed from the first day of the battle on entering Inf. work and this employment was justified by the seriousness of the situation. After the 23rd it was impossible to do any R.E. work as our tool carts had been sent back with the Divisional Transport –	

A6945 Wt. W11422/M1160 350,000 12/16 D. D. & L. Forms/C./2118/14.

Instructions regarding War Diaries and Intelligence Summaries are contained in F. S. Regs., Part II. and the Staff Manual respectively. Title pages will be prepared in manuscript.

17

WAR DIARY
or
INTELLIGENCE SUMMARY.
(Erase heading not required.)

Army Form C. 2118.

Place	Date	Hour	Summary of Events and Information	Remarks and references to Appendices
			March 1918	
			Up to the 26th many opportunities presented themselves for employment of R.E. profitably viz. [illegible] if the higher authorities could have given me some indication as to how far we were likely to withdraw, namely destruction of railways, destruction of wells, of small road bridges, felling trees across roads etc. ~~[illegible]~~ After troops were forced to withdraw from positions it was difficult for them to know where to reform and what position to take up, notably at BEAULIEU on the 23rd. The R.E. can be very usefully employed in helping to reform stragglers and to indicate the position for them to take up and if required by the senior officer present to assist in holding the position if there is no Divl area to the contrary. To carry out this work very close touch must be kept with the Division — On these rear positions dumps of S.A.A. & rations should be formed —	

E. C. [illegible] Maj R.E. (? Col)
O.C. 64 Fd Coy R.E.

[illegible] transport [illegible] are attached —

14th Div.

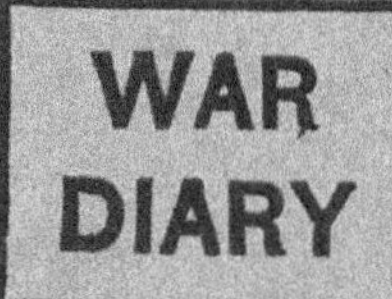

61st FIELD COMPANY, R.E.

A P R I L

1 9 1 8

Instructions regarding War Diaries and Intelligence Summaries are contained in F. S. Regs., Part II. and the Staff Manual respectively. Title pages will be prepared in manuscript.

WAR DIARY
or
INTELLIGENCE SUMMARY.
(Erase heading not required.)

Army Form C. 2118.

61 Fd Coy RE
Vol 36

Place	Date	Hour	Summary of Events and Information April 1918.	Remarks and references to Appendices
VELLENS	1st		Marched to FLECHY.	Ref.
FLECHY	2nd		" " VERS. where I met the C.R.E. who promised us at least one days rest if possible.	AMIENS 17.
VERS.	3rd	9.55 a.m.	Much to my disappointment I got orders to move to LONGEAU where I would receive orders as to my final destination. I left the transport in a gully 1/4 mile west of GLISSY and proceeded with the Coy to AUBIGNY where all the Coy spent the night in billets. The Division went into the line the same night in front of HAMEL.	
AUBIGNY	4th		Woken up at 5.30 a.m. by very heavy bombardment and so ~~[illegible]~~ gave orders for the Coy to "Stand To". About 9 a.m. C.R.E. came round to say that the 3 Coys had to move up to opp. Div. Hqs in FOUILLOY at 62D/O10b25 in form the last Div. reserve at the disposal of G.O.C. 14th Div. as the 11th Kings (Pioneers) had already gone up the line to take up a reserve position – At 11.30 a.m. it was decided that the R.E. would not be required to fight but to ~~[illegible]~~ man the rear line, then in an embryonic stage, stretching from river in O2.a.1.8. - Ry. O2c 1.5.	Sheet 62 D.

A6945 Wt. W11422/M1160 350,000 12/16 D. D. & L. Forms/C./2118/14.

Instructions regarding War Diaries and Intelligence Summaries are contained in F. S. Regs., Part II. and the Staff Manual respectively. Title pages will be prepared in manuscript.

WAR DIARY
or
INTELLIGENCE SUMMARY.
(Erase heading not required.)

Army Form C. 2118.

Place	Date	Hour	Summary of Events and Information	Remarks and references to Appendices
			April 1918.	
AUBIGNY.	4th		Ry O2C15 - Road O8c 8.5. - Track O14 b 3.3. - which was my section. The 89th Fd. Coy R.E. were on my right to Road O26 d 8.4.	
			In evening I received orders from C.R.E. to see General WINDSAR - B.G.C. 41st Inf Bde. and he told me to be ready to supply guides to put the remnants of 41st & 42nd Inf Bdes in the new line at 4.15 a.m. on the 5th. - This	
	5th		was done and after this the B.G.C. kept the 3 Field Coys in reserve at about O13 central.	
			Dug some new trenches on the line in the afternoon.	
BLANGY TROUVILLE			At night returned to billet in BLANGY TROUVILLE being at the tactical disposal of B.G.C. 41st Inf Bde.	
	6th		Built some shelters for Bn. Hqs. in bank in O13 b.	
	7th		Commenced wiring the front. - Completed 1250 yards. -	
			After work marched to billets at AMIENS with the Transport. -	
AMIENS.	8th		Capt HALLEY and all transport less 2 limbers & mess cart marched off under orders of O.C. 14th Div. Train.	
	9th		2 Lieut JONES marched with balance of Transport. -	

A6945 Wt. W11422/M1160 350,000 12/16 D. D. & L. Forms/C./2118/14.

Instructions regarding War Diaries and Intelligence Summaries are contained in F. S. Regs., Part II. and the Staff Manual respectively. Title pages will be prepared in manuscript.

3

Army Form C. 2118.

WAR DIARY
or
INTELLIGENCE SUMMARY.
(Erase heading not required.)

Place	Date	Hour	Summary of Events and Information	Remarks and references to Appendices
			April 1918.	
AMIENS	9th		During afternoon billets were shelled quite continually with H.V. shells & hence I considered it advisable to move to building ½ mile away where the 62nd Fd. Coy R.E. were billeted –	
YZRENGREMER	10th		Marched to & entrained at SALEUX ~~[illegible]~~ and detrained at GAMACHES at 3 p.m. whence marched to YZRENGREMER.	DIEPPE 16
	11th		Marched to & entrained at FEUQUIERES where all transport joined up. – Capt HALLEY having moved in 3 stages & 2 Lt TONES in 2 stages –	ABBEVILLE 14
WICQUINGHEM	12th		Detrained at MARESQUEL whence marched to WICQUINGHEM.	CALAIS 13.
	13th		Rested, cleaned up, drew some badly needed Ordnance Stores – Clothes ~~and~~ and boots all in very bad way	
	14th		3 Sect. bussed to MOLLINGHEM where I met C.R.E. ~~[illegible]~~ with whom I went over a rear G.H.Q. line on which work was to be commenced tomorrow. Coy & 1 section marched to MOLLINGHEM. This completes some 260 miles marching since 21st inst. –	
MOLLINGHEM	15th		Officers reconnoitred & taped out ~~Commenced~~ work on G.H.Q. line ~~[illegible]~~ –	
			This line consisted of some 4500x of front stretching from 36A. S.W. / O 11 c 3.2. through forward edge of CORNET BRASSART, forward edge of CORNET BOURDOIS to O 35 central for which front 62nd Fd. Coy R.E. worked – On the left 16th Div joined up	Sheet 36A. S.W.

A6945 Wt. W11422/M1160 350,000 12/16 D. D. & L. Forms/C./2118/14.

4

Instructions regarding War Diaries and Intelligence Summaries are contained in F. S. Regs., Part II. and the Staff Manual respectively. Title pages will be prepared in manuscript.

WAR DIARY
or
INTELLIGENCE SUMMARY.
(*Erase heading not required.*)

Army Form C. 2118.

Place	Date	Hour	Summary of Events and Information	Remarks and references to Appendices
			April 1918.	
MOLINGHEM	15th		The area in which the G.H.Q. line lay consisted of a very flat plain intersected by a few streams and many ditches many of which formed an appreciable obstacle to the passage of infantry — The water level generally was within 2 ft of the surface and in places it was impracticable to dig at all — Hence as a general ~~rule~~ types ~~type~~ which had to be adapted to the ground, following type of entrenchment was adopted —	
			By allowing 20'6" from the edge of the trench to the edge of the borrow pit allowance was made for the ultimate raising of parapet to 4'6" if required —	
			Sod revetment; 3/1; +3'; 4'6"; +3'; 1'6"; 1/2; borrow pit; 18"; 1'6"; 4'8"; 6'; 7'; 20'6"	
			Sod revetment was used throughout and proved very satisfactory —	
	16th		Commenced work with 400 men of 43rd Inf. Bde.	
	17th		Continued " " 1850 " " " " " —	
			Up to the 26th inst. 43rd Bde supplied between 1800 and 2100 men to work on this line — On the 25th 150 Portuguese Infantry were also given —	

A6945 Wt. W11422/M1160 350,000 12/16 D. D. & L. Forms/C./2118/14.

Instructions regarding War Diaries and Intelligence Summaries are contained in F. S. Regs., Part II. and the Staff Manual respectively. Title pages will be prepared in manuscript.

WAR DIARY
or
INTELLIGENCE SUMMARY.
(Erase heading not required.)

Place	Date	Hour	Summary of Events and Information April 1918.	Remarks and references to Appendices
MOLLINGHEM			On the 22nd a new forward line was commenced which included the defences of a bridgehead in 36A S.E.4 / P20 a & b and extended South along the road to P26a 3.9 – P26b 4.1 – P26a 6.6 P32a 5.8 to P32d 5.1. Some 4000 yds. The ground in this area was much the same as that in which the back line was being built but it was decided to make this line of a series of disconnected rifle posts of 2 firebays each on an average while the rear line was built as a continuous line with isolated supporting points.	
			On the forward line I received a working party of 1 Bn. about 550 men and this number was taken from those on the rear line.	
	26th		Only 150 Portuguese were available for work as the Bde left the area on the 27th.	
	27th		Carried on with the Coy and the Portuguese, who were only able to work on the rear line as the forward line was 7 miles from their billets.	

A6945 Wt. W11422/M1160 350,000 12/16 D. D. & L. Forms/C./2118/14.

Instructions regarding War Diaries and Intelligence Summaries are contained in F. S. Regs., Part II. and the Staff Manual respectively. Title pages will be prepared in manuscript.

or

INTELLIGENCE SUMMARY.

(Erase heading not required.)

Place	Date	Hour	April 1918 — Summary of Events and Information	Remarks and references to Appendices
MOLLINGHEM	30th		Reconnoitred bridgehead & defences of GUARBECQUE with G.O.C. & C.R.S.	Ref. AMIENS 17
			~~Ditto~~ At the end of the month the rear G.H.Q. line was wired throughout by a ~~single~~ double apron fence and round the salients comprising about 50% of the front with a second double apron fence. The continuous line had been commenced throughout the entire length and the parapet completed on about 75% of the front. Isolated support posts consisting generally of 2 firebays were completed in 15 instances. In order to provide depth to the system trenches to accommodate 2 Coys had been dug in BERGUETTE forming the nucleus of defence of the village.	8 Sheet 36A SE & S.W.
			The forward line in front of BUSNES had some 30% of the firebays completed and was wired throughout.	
			Considerable assistance was given by a voluntary working party ranging from 100 to 150 men of No 1 Special Coy R.E. who were billeted about O28 c8d and who worked on the Southern portion of the rear line.	

A6945 Wt. W11422/M1160 350,000 12/16 D. D. & L. Forms/C./2118/14.

Instructions regarding War Diaries and Intelligence Summaries are contained in F. S. Regs., Part II. and the Staff Manual respectively. Title pages will be prepared in manuscript.

~~WAR DIARY~~
or
INTELLIGENCE SUMMARY.
(Erase heading not required.)

Place	Date	Hour	Summary of Events and Information	Remarks and references to Appendices
			April 1918.	
HOLLINGHEM.			2nd Lieuts D. ELLISON R.S. & S. BURROWS R.S. and 20 O.R.s R.S. were attached to render assistance in the line of the Corps. The Sappers being mainly P.B. & "B" men could not only be employed in the work near Ypres as the majority could not stand the marching and a number were continually going sick.	
			Personnel:-	
	24th		2 Lieut. R.H. QUINTON R.E.(T) reported for duty from the Base	
			2 Lieut W.S. GOLDFINCH R.S.(T). do	
			2 Lieut C.G. CATCHPOLE R.E. (T.C.). do from sick leave	to U.K.
			E. C. Tempany Major R.E. (SR) O.C. 61st Fd Coy R.E.	

A6945 Wt. W11422/M1160 350,000 12/16 D. D. & L. Forms/C./2118/14.

Instructions regarding War Diaries and Intelligence Summaries are contained in F. S. Regs., Part II. and the Staff Manual respectively. Title pages will be prepared in manuscript.

WAR DIARY
or
INTELLIGENCE SUMMARY.
(Erase heading not required.)

Army Form C. 2118.

Vol 37

Place	Date	Hour	Summary of Events and Information May 1918.	Remarks and references to Appendices
MOLLINGHEM.	1st–6th		Worked on Rear G.H.Q. line from 011C 3.2. – CORNET BRASSART – CORNET BOURDOIS line known in future as the LILLERS – STEENBECQUE line with Port. Lab. Coy – strength about 150 – and some 100–150 voluntary workers of No 1 Coy Special Bde. R.E.	Sheet 36A SW & 36A SE. HAZEBROUCK 5A.
	7th		The 63rd, 79th, 87th Labour Coys – total of working strength about 300 – commenced work on LILLERS – STEENBECQUE line in addition to Port Lab. Coy. – The Special Bde ceased work.	
	8th		The 712th Lab. Coy worked on same line in addition to all parties on the 7th. Handed over all this line to O.C. 89th Fd. Coy. R.E.	
	1st–4th		Worked on BUSNES SWITCH with working parties of 1st Portuguese Field Coy – strength 140 – and 14th ~~Inf~~ Portuguese Inf. Bn – strength 500.	
	4th		Commenced work with 1 Coy of 14th Port Inf. Bn on a red front bridgehead at GUARBECQUE.	
	5th		Continued work on bridgehead and on new defences of GUARBECQUE with 1st Port. Fd. Coy and all the 14th Port. Inf. Bn. – The country in which these defences were made was very waterlogged so that generally it was	

A6945 Wt. W11422/M1160 350,000 12/16 D. D. & L. Forms/C./2118/14.

Instructions regarding War Diaries and Intelligence Summaries are contained in F. S. Regs., Part II. and the Staff Manual respectively. Title pages will be prepared in manuscript.

WAR DIARY
or
INTELLIGENCE SUMMARY.
(*Erase heading not required.*)

Army Form C. 2118.

Place	Date	Hour	Summary of Events and Information	Remarks and references to Appendices
			May. 1918 –	
			impossible to dig a trench ~~of~~ more than a foot deep.	Shts
HOLLINGHEM.	6th – 11th –		Worked on GUARBECQUE defences with No 4 Sect. attached R.E. under	36A S.W. 36A S.E.
			2Lt GOLDFINCH and No 3 after the 8th – and the 733rd & 159 Lab. Coys –	HAZEBROUCK 5.A –
	6th – 11th.		Worked on BUSNES SWITCH with Nos 1 & 2 Sect. with following parties –	
	6th		1st Port. Fd. Coy & 14th Port. Inf. Bn.	
	7th		" "	
	8th		" "	
	9th		" "	
	10th		" " + 23rd Port. Inf. Bn (good workers).	
	11th		" and 35th Port. Inf. Bn.	
	12th		No 2 Sect. and 50 % of 35 Port. Inf. Bn.	
	11th		Moved Nos 1 & 2 Sect. nearer their work to billets at LA PIERRIÈRE	
	13th		Hours of work increased to 8 hrs per day 8.0 am till noon & 12.30 pm – 4.30 pm.	
	13th – 18th		Worked on following points with working parties as shewn.	
			BUSNES SWITCH – Nos 1 & 2 Sections – 1st Portuguese Field Coy & 35th Portuguese Inf Bn	
			GUARBECQUE bridge head – No. 3 Section – 159th Labour Coy.	

A6945 Wt. W11422/M1160 350,000 12/16 D. D. & L. Forms/C./2118/14.

Instructions regarding War Diaries and Intelligence Summaries are contained in F. S. Regs., Part II. and the Staff Manual respectively. Title pages will be prepared in manuscript.

Army Form C. 2118.

WAR DIARY
or
INTELLIGENCE SUMMARY.
(Erase heading not required.)

Place	Date	Hour	Summary of Events and Information	Remarks and references to Appendices
			May 1918.	
MOLLINGHEM	13th-18th		GUARBECQUE defences — No 4 Section (attached section) of 733rd Labour Coy.	
			MAIN LINE 2 or 3 sappers from attached section + Portuguese Labour Cy.	
	19th		Inter company horse show + inspection of transport at HAM-EN-ARTOIS.	
			Condition of horses was not very good owing to several cases of sand cholic	
	20th	8.0am	H.V shell fell in transport lines killing one driver + eight horses +	
			wounding one driver + 3 horses of whom one had to be shot.	
			Practised "MAN BATTLE STATIONS." The company held the main	Sheet 36A S.W.
			LILLERS STEENBECQUE line from O.11.c.2.0 to O.28.b.65	66.
			Practice finished about 11.0 am + normal work was resumed.	
	21st		The road through MOLLINGHEM was shelled for a short time. One	
			shell fell in the yard at headquarters billet + killed Sergt CLARKE	
			3rd Portuguese M.G. Group commenced work on BUSNES SWITCH.	
			Transport moved to OBLOIS WOOD between MOLLINGHEM and MAZINGHEM	
	22nd-27th		Work the same as from the 13th with the addition of the Portuguese M.G. Group on the	
			BUSNES SWITCH.	
	28th		Work the same as the 27th. Took over portion of main LILLERS-STEENBECQUE	

A6945 Wt. W11422/M1160 350,000 12/16 D. D. & L. Forms/C./2118/14.

Instructions regarding War Diaries and Intelligence Summaries are contained in F. S. Regs., Part II. and the Staff Manual respectively. Title pages will be prepared in manuscript.

WAR DIARY
or
INTELLIGENCE SUMMARY.
(Erase heading not required.)

Army Form C. 2118.

Place	Date	Hour	Summary of Events and Information	Remarks and references to Appendices
			May 1918.	
MOLLINGHEM	28th cont		defensive system from Lt. Col FALCON DSO R.E. Front line boundary of portion taken over from O.11.c.2.0 to I 33 d.8.3.	Sheet 36a SW + 36a N.W.
	29th		Commenced work on line taken over on 28th. Distribution of work as follows:-	
			Nos 1 + 2 Sections on BUSNES SWITCH working parties 1st Portuguese Field Coy + 35th Portuguese Inf Battn.	
			No 4 + attached sections on main LILLERS - STEENBECQUE line the same as on 28th with the addition of Portuguese M.G. Coy as working party.	
			No 3 section on GUARBECQUE bridge head with the same working party as on 28th.	
			On new line following officers + O.R were employed, 4 RE officers + 45 O.R. 11th Hants (Pioneers) 1 officer + 23 O.R. Working Parties 1 Portuguese Battn Inf, 1 M.G. Coy Portuguese, 1 Coy Portuguese Pioneers	
	30th		Work the same as the 29th.	
	31st		Took over line from I 33 d 8 3 to I.22.c.3.1 from 157th Field Coy. R.E. + commenced work on it with the attached R.E.	
			No. 4 section took over line from O.11.c.2.0. Northwards to canal bank + No 3 section took over from canal bank to O.5.d.0.8. from attached R.E.s	
			89th Field Coy R.E. took over portion of main LILLERS - STEENBECQUE from South of BERGUETTE - GUARBECQUE road, + Portuguese Labour Coy + 154th Labour Coy + 2 sections who were working on GUARBECQUE BRIDGEHEAD under No 3 section.	
			Remainder of work as for 30th.	

D. D. & L., London, E.C. (A8004) Wt. W1771/M2731 750,000 5/17 Sch. 52 Forms/C2118/14

Army Form C. 2118.

Instructions regarding War Diaries and Intelligence Summaries are contained in F. S. Regs., Part II. and the Staff Manual respectively. Title pages will be prepared in manuscript.

WAR DIARY
or
INTELLIGENCE SUMMARY.
(Erase heading not required.)

Place	Date	Hour	Summary of Events and Information	Remarks and references to Appendices
			May 1918.	
MOLINGHEM			Honours:-	
			O.C. MAJOR E.E.V. TEMPERLEY R.E.S.R. awarded bar to M.C. D.R.O. 1147 of 6.5.18.	
			No 488491. Cpl. H.B. WEBB awarded M.M	
			No 154710. Spr. E.G. McGUINNESS " D.R.O. ~~D~~ 1147 of 6.5.18.	

E. E. V. Temperley
MAJOR R. E. (S. R.)
O. C. 61st FIELD COY, R. E.

D. D. & L., London, E.C.
(A8004) Wt. W1771/M2 31 750,000 5/17 Sch. 52 Forms/C2118/14

29

Instructions regarding War Diaries and Intelligence Summaries are contained in F. S. Regs., Part II. and the Staff Manual respectively. Title pages will be prepared in manuscript.

WAR DIARY
or
INTELLIGENCE SUMMARY.
(Erase heading not required.)

Army Form C. 2118.

JUNE. 1918.

9/R 38

61st Fd Co R.E.

Place	Date	Hour	Summary of Events and Information Ref. 36A & HAZEBROUCK. 5A.	Remarks and references to Appendices
MOLLINGEM	1st –		Worked on LILLERS – STEEN BECQUE Line from 017a5.2 – I 22d07.71 –	
			with following labour. (av. strength 421)	
			British:– 733rd Lab. Coy, ~~all Companies~~ 6th Bn. Leinsters (12th – 15th) – (av. strength 330)	
			attached R.E. "B" Category – 66 O.R. – 2 Coys R.I.R. attached 8th K.R.R.C. (av 170) from 20th	
			Portuguese:– 4th Port. Fd. Cy. (strength about 70).	
			21st Port. Inf. Bn (av. strength 410).	
			34th Port. Inf. Bn (do 420)	
			Port. Pioneers (do 150).	
			2nd Port M.G. Coy (do 55) Employed solely on the STEEL WORKS –	
			1st Port Lab. Coy (do 180) from 10th to 12th –	
			3rd Port M.G. Cy (do 55). up to 10th.	
			Also Worked on RESERVE Line South of THIENNES –	
			Labour – 1st Port. Lab. Cy. from 12th.	
			Also worked on deepening of the trenches in vicinity of M.T. CORBEAU – 086.	
			Labour – 5th Companies – from 12th – 25th	
			Type of breastwork constructed was as shown in attached print –	
			Tasks on breastworks were allotted as shown in attached print –	
			Type of trenches dug as in attached pamphlet –	
			The management of the Portuguese labour presented great difficulties as	
			their one object (with the exception of the Field Coys.) was to do as little	

D. D. & L., London, E.C. (A8004) Wt. W1771/M2 31 750,000 5/17 Sch. 52 Forms/C2118/14

Instructions regarding War Diaries and Intelligence Summaries are contained in F. S. Regs., Part II. and the Staff Manual respectively. Title pages will be prepared in manuscript.

2

WAR DIARY
or
INTELLIGENCE SUMMARY.
(Erase heading not required.)

Army Form C. 2118.

61st Fd Coy RE

Place	Date	Hour	Summary of Events and Information — JUNE 1918.	Remarks and references to Appendices
MOLLINGHEM			work as possible with the result that it was found impossible to employ them on sod revetment as part of a task because the revetment would be so badly done as to be simply useless – But if a reasonable task of about 100 cu. feet of filling up on a breastwork was allotted they would work like maniacs and get it completed in 3½ hours or less – If a bigger task was allotted they would sulk and take an inordinate time in completing the task – By careful supervision and great help from the British training Offrs. it was possible to get about 100 cu. feet done. The Port. Field Coys were a great help and are highly skilled in Field Works but the Port. Infantry Offrs. are a little inclined to lack common sense and so require a good deal of supervision –	

D. D. & L., London, E.C. (A8004) Wt. W1771/M2 31 750,000 5/17 Sch. 52 Forms/C2118/14

Instructions regarding War Diaries and Intelligence Summaries are contained in F. S. Regs., Part II. and the Staff Manual respectively. Title pages will be prepared in manuscript.

3.

WAR DIARY
or
INTELLIGENCE SUMMARY.
(Erase heading not required.)

Army Form C. 2118.

61st Fd Coy RE

Place	Date	Hour	Summary of Events and Information	Remarks and references to Appendices
			JUNE – 1918.	
MOLLINGHEM.	1st –		Work on the BUSNES SWITCH from P20b 20.15 – P32a 80.45 was continued up to 10th when the work was handed over to O.C. 62nd Ry Coy RE. Labour:– 1st Port Fd. Coy average strength 60. 35th Port Inf. Bn do 200 It was found that – Pure breastworks are completed at the rate of 1 man does 1 yard in 6 days. 10 Sp. can erect hurdle revetment to supply 200 Infantry with work. The following work was carried out on 18th at request of Corps. The culvert at MAZINGHEM Cross Roads was reported to require repairs and on inspection it was found that the centre portion for a length of 22'6" was in a very dangerous state and beyond repair. Traffic considerations rendered it important to complete the work in the shortest possible time and the road was reopened for traffic after 14½ hours work. Working Party:– 16 R.E. 33 Lab. Coy. Sketches showing work carried out. →	

9" Brick arch — Pavé — Road Level — 2' — 3' — 7'6" — OLD BRIDGE

Filling of Rubble & Road metal — Existing Brick wall — 3' — 7'6" — NEW BRIDGE

[illegible]
Maj R.E.(Cdg)
O.C. 61st Fd Coy R.E.
30.6.18

D. D. & L., London, E.C. (A8004) Wt. W1771/M2 31 750,000 5/17 Sch. 52 Forms/C2118/14

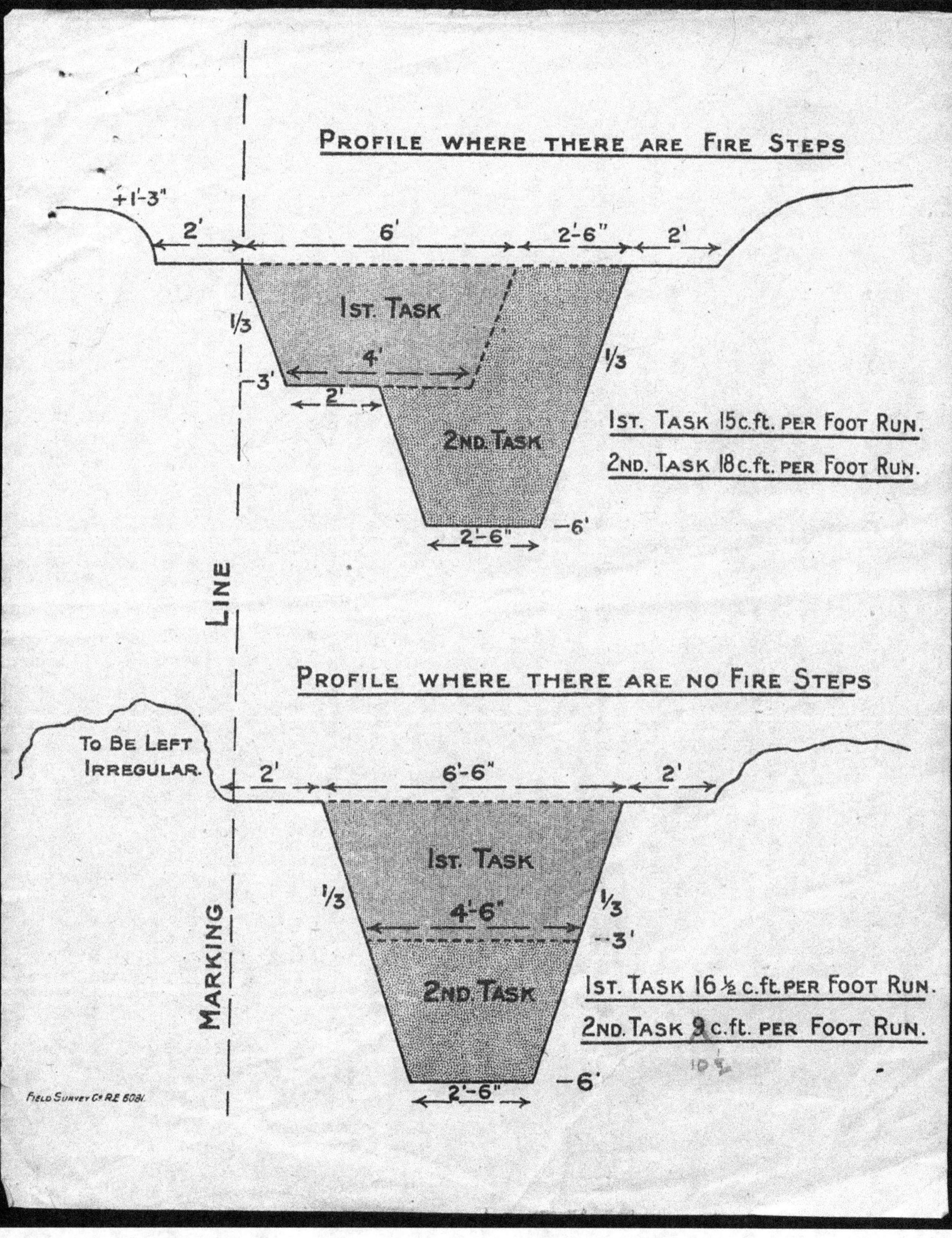

Profile where there are Fire Steps
+1'-3"
2'
6'
2'-6"
2'
1st. Task
1/3
4'
1/3
-3'
2'
2nd. Task
1st. Task 15 c.ft. per Foot Run.
2nd. Task 18 c.ft. per Foot Run.
-6'
2'-6"
Marking Line
Profile where there are no Fire Steps
To Be Left Irregular.
2'
6'-6"
2'
1st. Task
1/3
1/3
4'-6"
-3'
2nd. Task
1st. Task 16½ c.ft. per Foot Run.
2nd. Task 9 c.ft. per Foot Run.
-6'
2'-6"
Field Survey Cº R.E. 6081.

Instructions for the preparation of Emergency Defensive Lines

FIRST ARMY.

1. The Trace.—This should consist of a continuous Line of Resistance, to be sited in front of the crest in order to obtain observation and to deny observation to the enemy A Piquet Line should be 100 to 150 yards in front of the Line of Resistance and a Reserve Line 300 to 400 yards behind it. The latter should, when possible, be out of view of the enemy. These two lines need not be continuous, but all trenches intended for occupation must be joined to the Line of Resistance by Communication Trenches. These should not be perpendicular to the general line, but so traced as to be available as switches.

It saves time and labor if the trace is ploughed instead of being taped. Six furrows are sufficient to break the surface.

The trace will generally be of the waved type. The length of waves may be varied from 70′ to 100′ to suit the ground. The perpendicular distance from the chord to the inside bend will vary in proportion from 16′ to 30′. Traverses 16′ thick should be given where the trench is likely to be definitely enfiladed.

2. The Profile.—The Profile will be as per accompanying sketches. Firebays will be given in about 50 per cent. of the line. They should generally be 18′ long to accommodate 8 rifles, and should be sited when possible to fill the minor undulations of the ground.

3. Order of Work.—

1. Piquet Line first task.
2. Line of Resistance first task.
3. Line of Resistance second task.
4. Communications.
5. Piquet Line second task.
6. Reserve Line first task.
7. Communications.
8. Reserve Line second task.

The Piquet Line will be the line to be wired.

4. Organisation of Work.—Definite tasks must be allotted to units and sub-units. Unit Commanders will be held responsible that the allotted tasks are completed, and that as soon as completed the troops are dismissed. No unit having finished its task will ever be kept to complete that of another unit. Disciplinary action must be taken should any unit be dismissed without completing its task.

The size of task allotted per man will be fixed by the Officer in charge of the works, varying with the nature of the soil, the class and duties of the man.

5. Wire.—Wire is at present scarce. In the first instance a belt of wire will be placed in an irregular line of 40 to 50 yards in front of the Piquet Line.

This belt will consist of a double apron fence, with two bays of medium wire entanglement in front of it, 3′ high and lightly festooned so as to form a definite obstacle which a man cannot walk over, and cut the strands of the apron fence with his rifle attachment. If time and material permit further belts will be placed in front and distances varying from 30 to 50 yards. Belts must not be parallel to each other, and must be of irregular trace. All wire must be covered by rifle or machine gun fire.

First Army,
7-4-18.

E. ATKINSON, *Major-General,*
Chief Engineer, First Army.

[P.T.O.

Breastwork Task Diagram (with Hurdle Revetment)

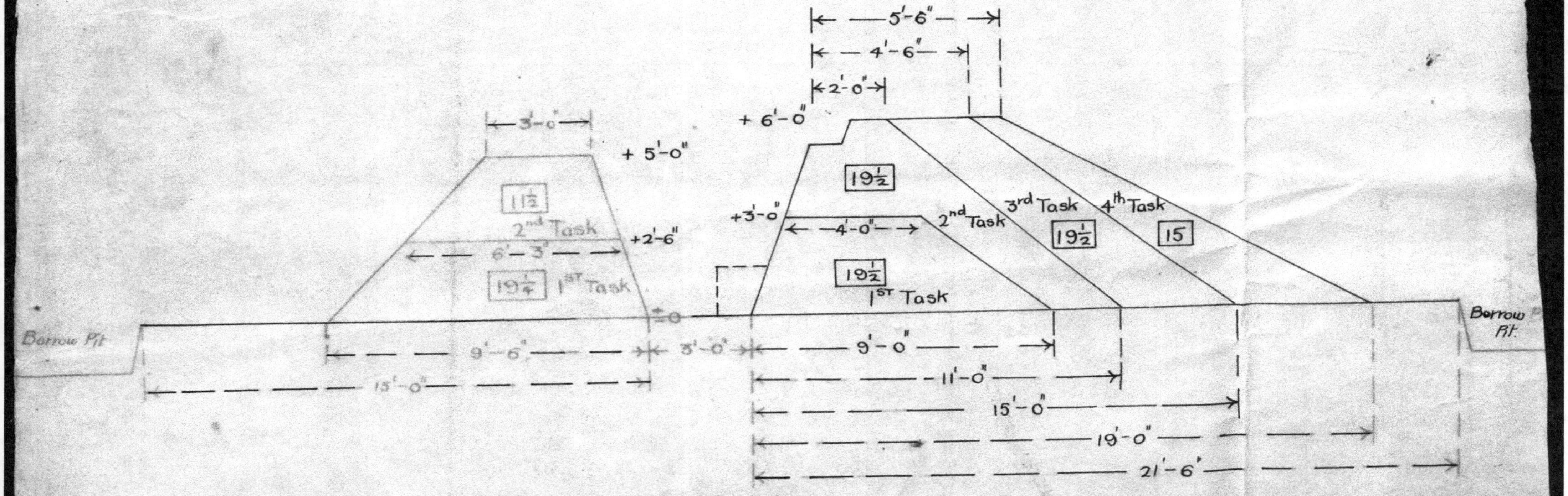

3'-0"
+ 5'-0"
$11\frac{1}{2}$
2nd Task
+2'-6"
6'-3"
$19\frac{1}{4}$ 1st Task
±0
Borrow Pit
9'-6"
3'-0"
15'-0"

5'-6"
4'-6"
2'-0"
+ 6'-0"
$19\frac{1}{2}$
+3'-0"
4'-0"
2nd Task
3rd Task
4th Task
$19\frac{1}{2}$
15
$19\frac{1}{2}$
1st Task
Borrow Pit
9'-0"
11'-0"
15'-0"
19'-0"
21'-6"

Numbers shown thus $19\frac{1}{2}$ indicate Cubic Feet of Earth per foot run of Breastwork

61st Fld Co. R.E.

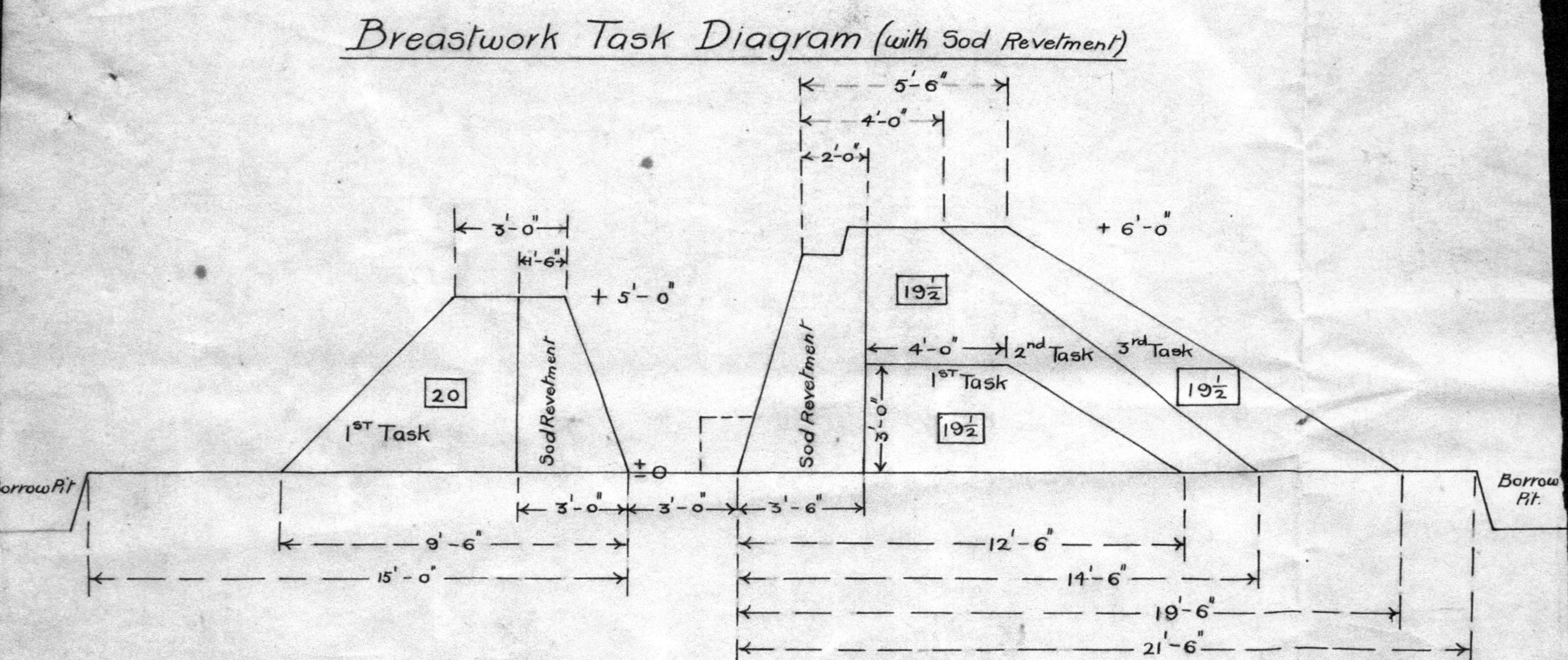
Breastwork Task Diagram (with Sod Revetment)
5'-6"
4'-0"
2'-0"
3'-0"
1'-6"
+ 5'-0"
+ 6'-0"
20
1st Task
Sod Revetment
19½
4'-0"
2nd Task
3rd Task
1st Task
19½
19½
3'-0"
±0
Borrow Pit
Borrow Pit
3'-0"
3'-0"
3'-6"
9'-6"
15'-0"
12'-6"
14'-6"
19'-6"
21'-6"
Numbers shown thus 19½ indicate Cubic Feet of Earth per foot run of Breastwork
61st Fld.Co.R.

Dimensions of Breastworks

Semi-Breastwork (when Sods not available)

Scale :- 8 ft = 1 in

Firebay

Enemy →

Borrow Pit

Traverse

Slope Slightly Steeper than 3/1

Borrow Pit

Semi-Breastwork (when Sods are available)

Scale :- 8 ft = 1 in

Firebay

Enemy →

Borrow Pit

Traverse

Slope slightly steeper than 3/1

Borrow Pit

Breastwork with Firestep

Scale :- 8 ft = 1 in

Firebay

Enemy →

Hurdles

Wire

Borrow Pit

Traverse

Slope Slightly Steeper than 3/1

Hurdles

Wire

Borrow Pit

If, Sods are used Dimensions will be as above, except that slope of Sod Revetment will be 3/1

NOTES:-

1. If Deeper Trench than 1'6" can be Dug, Breastwork will be lowered accordingly.
2. Excavation of Borrow Pit will be commenced at greatest distance from Trench that it is calculated earth will be required from.
3. Behind Alternate Traverses Gaps will be left in Parados.

61st Fld. Co. R.E.

Instructions regarding War Diaries and Intelligence Summaries are contained in F. S. Regs., Part II. and the Staff Manual respectively. Title pages will be prepared in manuscript.

WAR DIARY
or
INTELLIGENCE SUMMARY.
(Erase heading not required.)

JULY 1918

Army Form C. 2118.

61st FIELD COMPANY ROYAL ENGINEERS Date 2.8.18

Vol 39

Place	Date	Hour	Summary of Events and Information	Remarks and references to Appendices
MOLINGHEM	1st to 8th		Continued work on LILLERS-STEENBECQUE line as during June, but without the [illegible] regiments which left the district. Reconstruction of old French trenches breastworks on reserve line S. of THIENNES was carried out; & some work was done on the repair of trenches on the front line of the MT. CORBEAU system; both of these with Portugese labour. Work on the STEEL WORKS was completed	
	8th		Received orders to march the following day to SETQUES, & from there to proceed to rejoin the Division at WIERRE EFFROY.	
	9th		Moved to SETQUES – after arriving there received orders to remain there & await instructions	
SETQUES	10th 11th		Remained at SETQUES; on the 11th got orders to move on the 12th to rejoin the division at WESTROVE	
	12th		Moved to WESTROVE – good billets.	
WESTROVE	to 28th		At EPERLECQUES (WESTROVE billeting area). Work consisted mainly of training – infantry drill, musketry etc, with a certain amount of work for the Division, re camps etc.	
	25th		The Company was inspected by G.O.C. Division, who commented very favourably on the turnout & appearance of men & transport	
	29th		Moved to LONGUENESSE	
	30th		" " EBBLINGHEM	
	31st		Arrived at EECKHOUTE CASTEEL for work under XV Corps	

F. A. A. Richmond Capt R.E.
O/C 61st Fd Company

D. D. & L. London, E.C. (A8034) Wt. W1771/M2 31 750,000 5/17 Sch. 52 Forms/C2118/14

Instructions regarding War Diaries and Intelligence Summaries are contained in F. S. Regs., Part II. and the Staff Manual respectively. Title pages will be prepared in manuscript.

WAR DIARY
or
INTELLIGENCE SUMMARY.

(Erase heading not required.)

Army Form C. 2118.

WR 40

Place	Date	Hour	AUGUST 1918 Summary of Events and Information	Remarks and references to Appendices
EECK HOUT CASTEEL	1st		Took over work on EAST HAZEBROUCK LINE	
	2nd		Commenced work. Labour consisted of 6th, 13th & 133rd Labour Coys. which averaged about 240 working strength per company. The work consisted of wiring, trenches, breastwork & semi-breastwork, according to the lie of the land: L. G. posts: clearing hedges & cutting crops: putting in splinter proof shelters: & draining, which was a matter of considerable importance. For the first six days all work was done on the front line - after that it was all concentrated on the support line. The type of wire adopted was three belts of double apron fence at about 20x intervals split up into compartments by cross belts. The supply of material was good.	
	16th		Moved to DROGLANDT Area - billets & bivouacs	
DROGLANDT area	17th		Moved to PROVEN - Nissen hut camp	
PROVEN	18th		Moved to BENWELL CAMP - PESELHOEK - came under orders of C.E. II Corps, for work on VLAMERTINGHE LINE	
BENWELL CAMP	19th		Took over work from O.C. 208th & 209th Fd Coys.	
"	20th		Moved to G 4 d 7.3. Sheet 28 and built a camp there.	

D. D. & L., London, E.C. (A8004) Wt. W1771/M2 31 750,000 5/17 Sch. 52 Forms/C2118/14

Instructions regarding War Diaries and Intelligence Summaries are contained in F. S. Regs., Part II. and the Staff Manual respectively. Title pages will be prepared in manuscript.

WAR DIARY
or
INTELLIGENCE SUMMARY.
(Erase heading not required.)

Army Form C. 2118.

Place	Date	Hour	Summary of Events and Information	Remarks and references to Appendices
	21st		Started work on VLAMERTINGHE LINE. Work consisted of building shelters of the pyramid type - framework of pit-props & 9"x3" scantling, C.I. walls, roof of steel rails covered with corrugating - then 3' of earth, then a burster course of bricks, then another 6' of earth then another brick burster, just covered with earth. One section R.E. was employed on each of three shelters, the sappers had to do the whole of the work, no working parties being supplied - this resulted in a great waste of skilled labour, as at least 75% of the work was earth shovelling.	
	28th		Moved to Sheet 28 - H12 a 3.5. & took over work in the line from 208th Fd Coy. HQrs & 2 sections were at this map reference & two sections in forward billets	

F. H. A. Richmond
Capt R.E.
a/O.C. 61st Fd Coy R.E.

D. D. & L., London, E.C. (A8004) Wt. W1771/M2 31 750,000 5/17 Sch. 52 Forms/C2118/14

Instructions regarding War Diaries and Intelligence Summaries are contained in F. S. Regs., Part II. and the Staff Manual respectively. Title pages will be prepared in manuscript.

WAR DIARY
or
INTELLIGENCE SUMMARY.
(Erase heading not required.)

61st FIELD COMPANY Date 1.10.18 ROYAL ENGINEERS

Army Form C. 2118.

Place	Date	Hour	September 1918. Summary of Events and Information	Remarks and references to Appendices
H12 a 3.5.	1st–18th.		2 Sections were employed in the Intermediate Area i.e. round and about Bde Hqrs H5c.9.9. and the BROWN LINE – This work consisted of Erecting Bomb-proof shelters in the Support Line of the Brown Line, ditto round ECONOME HOUSE – H11a8.6 –, Building concrete walls to Bde. Major's office, concrete walls & roof to other Bde Quarters & offs., building concrete shelter for Bn. Hqrs., & improving the cover on quarters in Bde. Hqrs, erecting 1 MOIR PILL Box	Sheet 28.
	5th.		Took over from Lt BROWNE R.E. the demolition charges at LILLE GATE, I13c 95.50, I13a 7.4., I7c 45.70, & at I12c 6.6. at which places I had maintained Sappers to guard and to act – The charge at I13a.7.4. under a bridge over the YPRES COMMINES CANAL had been withdrawn for inspection and testing of the ammonal – The testing of the ammonal was completed and I gave orders for its replacement.	
	6th		The N.C.O. i/c had completed the fixing of the 50 lb tins in the wooden case when suddenly the whole charge exploded leaving no trace of the N.C.O. & the 2 Sappers assisting. –	

D. D. & L., London, E.C. (A8004) Wt. W1771/M2 31 750,000 5/17 Sch. 52 Forms/C2118/14

Instructions regarding War Diaries and Intelligence Summaries are contained in F. S. Regs., Part II. and the Staff Manual respectively. Title pages will be prepared in manuscript.

WAR DIARY
or
INTELLIGENCE SUMMARY.
(Erase heading not required.)

Army Form C. 2118.

Place	Date	Hour	September 1918. Summary of Events and Information	Remarks and references to Appendices
1st–18th H12a 3.5 YPRES–			Worked with 43rd Inf. Bde in the line who were holding a front from a point some 400x South of ZILLEBEKE LAKE to a point some 700x North of same –	Sheet 28.
			Two Sections were worked in forward zone and lived on Island at I 14 a 5 2 and whose work consisted of items as below.	
			Revetting, building up, & drainage of Support line.	
			Erecting Bay Elephant Shelters in " "	
			Draining ~~Support~~ Front line –	
			Miscellaneous items such as fixing gas curtains, maintenance of tramway, repair of Infantry Bridges across the Moat, repair of baths & pumps, and preparation of site for concrete dugout just outside LILLE GATE –	
			WARRINGTON Road – a double width planked road – was repaired in 3 nights by 2 Sect. from its inception to the front line for traffic in one direction – a distance of 3000x – Road had been badly damaged & the nights were not quiet –	

D. D. & L., London, E.C.
(A8004) Wt. W1771/M2 31 750,000 5/17 Sch. 52 Forms/C2118/14

Instructions regarding War Diaries and Intelligence Summaries are contained in F. S. Regs., Part II. and the Staff Manual respectively. Title pages will be prepared in manuscript.

3/

WAR DIARY
or
INTELLIGENCE SUMMARY.
(Erase heading not required.)

Army Form C. 2118.

Place	Date	Hour	Summary of Events and Information	Remarks and references to Appendices
			September 1918.	
H12a3.5.	5.		No satisfactory solution of this explosion has been arrived at – alternative theories are that the charge, which consisted of 400 lbs of ammonal was detonated, was exploded by a shell and the other that the ammonium nitrate in the ammonal had attacked the copper of the detonators & rendered them unsafe to handle. This explosion seriously damaged the civilian girder bridge & the East abutment and entirely destroyed the military wooden trestle bridge built to carry all loads less tanks and consisting of 7 trestles at 11 ft centres covering a clear span of This bridge was reconstructed from salved material from the old bridge and elsewhere & was practically completed except for the decking before handing over. This was not considered a specially urgent work & so no special arrangements were made to complete quickly and also the Corps could not supply any material to reconstruct it –	

D. D. & L., London, E.C. (A8004) Wt. W1771/M2·31 750,000 5/17 Sch. 52 Forms/C2118/14

Instructions regarding War Diaries and Intelligence Summaries are contained in F. S. Regs., Part II. and the Staff Manual respectively. Title pages will be prepared in manuscript.

4

WAR DIARY
or
INTELLIGENCE SUMMARY.

(Erase heading not required.)

Army Form C. 2118.

Place	Date	Hour	Summary of Events and Information — September 1918.	Remarks and references to Appendices
	19th		Handed over to 455th Fd. Coy R.E. 29th Div –	
			Coy transport moved by Lt Rly and transport by road to BUSSEBOOM –	
BUSSEBOOM.	20 – 27th		Worked on Div. Hqrs, erecting huts, latrines, cookhouse, fittings etc. improvements to A.D.S.	
			making forward Div. Hqrs at HAGUE FARM 28/H25c7.0.	
			making a dry weather mule track from DICKEBUSCH, thro' RIDGE WOOD to point 300x behind front line at BUS HOUSE at 28/O2a 3.7.	
	Night of 25 – 26		Whilst engaged on the last named work No 3 Section and 2nd Lieut QUINTON were assembly near BUS HOUSE before going home when suddenly the Germans raided our line with about 100 men. The front line posts did not stop the raid and about 50 Germans were seen coming across country preceded by a man who came running down shouting "Don't fire the Lancashires are retiring". As the Germans approached within about 30 yards Lt QUINTON challenged them and they replied "Lancashires" and immediately opened fire with rifles and bombs.	

D. D. & L., London, E.C. (A8004) Wt. W1771/M2·31 750,000 5/17 Sch. 52 Forms/C2118/14

5

Instructions regarding War Diaries and Intelligence Summaries are contained in F. S. Regs., Part II. and the Staff Manual respectively. Title pages will be prepared in manuscript.

WAR DIARY
or
INTELLIGENCE SUMMARY.

(Erase heading not required.)

Army Form C. 2118.

Place	Date	Hour	September 1918. Summary of Events and Information	Remarks and references to Appendices
	27th		The Sappers returned the fire but were driven back to the support line. Casualties were 1 off wounded, 4 O.R. wounded. 2 OR wounded & prisoner, 2 O.R. missing believed prisoner. 1 off & 17 O.R. had occupied the post.	
	27th		H.qrs. and 4 Sec. moved up to ~~[illegible]~~ a forward position in MELTON COPSE in 28/H26b	
	28th		attack of Belgians and Second Army at 5.30 a.m. The work allotted to R.E. & Pioneers was to make good the VOORMEZEELE – ST ELOI – EIKOF FM – HOLLEBEKE Road as far forward as the conditions would allow. The 1st shift consisted of 67 Fd Coy R.E. "C" Coy & 2 plats of "B" Coy of 15th L.N. Lancs (Pioneers) and on receipt of orders from C.R.E. they moved off their posts at 10 a.m. A convoy of wagons loaded with planks etc. which was waiting at PIONEER DUMP (28/H16 d 1.1.) under Capt RICHMOND moved off at same time. The attack was very successful & hence enemy retaliation was slight and by the end of 1st shift the road was through for horse transport up to ST. ELOI. Tank traps at ST ELOI were found & removed –	

D. D. & L., London, E.C. (A8004) Wt. W1771/M2 31 750,000 5/17 Sch. 52 Forms/C2118/14

Instructions regarding War Diaries and Intelligence Summaries are contained in F. S. Regs., Part II. and the Staff Manual respectively. Title pages will be prepared in manuscript.

6.

WAR DIARY
or
INTELLIGENCE SUMMARY.
(Erase heading not required.)

Army Form C. 2118.

Place	Date	Hour	Summary of Events and Information — September 1918	Remarks and references to Appendices
	28.		Owing to presence of enemy M.Gs on the DAMN STRASSE it was impossible to work East of the crest at ST ELOI.	
			62. Fd. Coy R.E. & 1½ Coys of Pioneers worked on second shift.	
	29.		Continued work on road and got thro' to DAMN STRASSE.	
			Reconnoitred road to HOLLEBEKE which was a German plank road and in most places not seriously damaged.	
			The second shift expected road thro' to HOLLEBEKE.	
			Moved to forward camp near CAFE BELGE.	
	30.		Continued work on road.	
			Full detonated charges ~~[illegible] YPRES~~ in bridges over YPRES-COMINES Canal at 28/O.12 b 4.6 were discovered and removed.	
			Charges consisted of 2 100 lb medium T.M. shells on the top of the transoms on each of 2 of the wooden trestles in each bridge.	
			Charges were arranged to be fired both electrically & by time fuze. The German exploder in the shape of a dry cell was also discovered.	
			1.10.18. E. C. W. [signature]	

D. D. & L., London, E.C. (A8004) Wt. W1771/M2-31 750,000 5/17 Sch. 52 Forms/C2118/14

Instructions regarding War Diaries and Intelligence Summaries are contained in F. S. Regs., Part II. and the Staff Manual respectively. Title pages will be prepared in manuscript.

WAR DIARY
or
INTELLIGENCE SUMMARY.
(Erase heading not required.)

Army Form C. 2118.

61 Fd Co RE
Vol 42

Place	Date	Hour	Summary of Events and Information — October 1918	Remarks and references to Appendices
	1st		Stood by to move but no orders received –	
	2nd		Coy & Transport moved to 28/T11 d 0.4.	
	3rd		Worked on road with 1/2 Coy Pioneers from T10 a 9.3 – T11 c 8 d – T24 a 89	
	4th – 13th		Worked on repairing above road & WULVERGHEM – MESSINES Road until 10th when the Pioneers took over the work. Also erected Bde Hqs for 42nd Inf. Bde & 43rd Inf. Bde. Both these consisted of 3 NISSEN Huts & usual offices & were completed in 3 days – An old barn, [struck out] in a state of bad disrepair, at NEUVE EGLISE was fitted up as a bath house, baths fixed, clean & dirty clothes stores lined, stove fixed up, by 1 Sect in 2 days –	
	12th – 13th		Replaced a hastily built bridge at 28/T36 3.2 by a bridge to take all loads. The [struck out] hastily built bridge was built in 2 parts and one half was rebuilt at a time in order to avoid stopping the traffic. This was done by 2 32 Spns working 18½ hrs in shifts of 6 hrs. A good deal of extra excavation was entailed owing to the excessive length of the only girders supplied – Sketch attached marked D.	
	14th		Work was suspended on the 14th owing to Coy standing by for the battle –	

D. D. & L., London, E.C. (A8004) Wt. W1771/M2031 750,000 5/17 Sch. 52 Forms/C2118/14

2

Instructions regarding War Diaries and Intelligence Summaries are contained in F. S. Regs., Part II. and the Staff Manual respectively. Title pages will be prepared in manuscript.

WAR DIARY
or
INTELLIGENCE SUMMARY.
(Erase heading not required.)

Army Form C. 2118.

Place	Date	Hour	October – 1918 – Summary of Events and Information	Remarks and references to Appendices
	15th		At 12 noon the Coy moved upon lorries to ~~SAILORS CROS~~ MESSINES and marched to SAILOR'S CROSSING (28/V26 9.8.) in order to take over work from 89th Fd Coy R.E. who had arranged to place 4 footbridges across the LYS and the Infantry had established a bridgehead — I received orders from C.R.E. to place a pontoon bridge across the LYS at 28/V26 9.8. & he placed the bridging equipment of the 3 Field Coys at my disposal — at 16.00 hrs the first pontoon in the water & by 21.00 hrs the bridge was open — 4 pontoons & 3 trestles were used — The approaches presented great difficulty as the old approach to a pile bent bridge was about ~~20~~ 12' above water level & hence was useless for a pontoon bridge & consequently a diversion had to be made on to the original roadway — At the same time the footbridges at 28/V4 a.20., 28/P35 d 0.3, 28/P36 a 2.8. were remade & improved —	

D. D. & L., London, E.C.
(A8004) Wt. W1771/M2-31 750,000 5/17 Sch. 52 Forms/C2118/14

Instructions regarding War Diaries and Intelligence Summaries are contained in F. S. Regs., Part II. and the Staff Manual respectively. Title pages will be prepared in manuscript.

~~2~~ 3

WAR DIARY
or
INTELLIGENCE SUMMARY.
(Erase heading not required.)

Army Form C. 2118.

Place	Date	Hour	October 1918 Summary of Events and Information	Remarks and references to Appendices
COMINES	16th		Completed causeway from old causeway to bridgehead, a length of 600'. Footbridge repaired & made good. Reconnaissance made of main bridge in COMINES. The traffic on the pontoon bridge was immense as this bridge was the only heavy traffic bridge for several miles up & down the LYS.	
	17th		Commenced repair at 06.30 hrs on MORTE LYS Bridge at COMINES by 9th GOLDFINCH & NOK Cos. and 6 Australians. Commenced at making a lorry bridge across the LOCK GATE at 12.00 hrs.	Sketch of bridge attached marked "A" & notes. A
	18th		Completed MORTE LYS Bridge at 08.30 hrs to take 7 ton axle load. The bridge had a clear span of 53'. 3 spans of which had to be reconstructed involving the repair of 3 missing damaged pile bents. LOCK GATE Bridge opened for traffic, 7 tons axle load at 15.35 hrs. This bridge had a clear span of 90' with 4 spans. Only 1 trestle had to be erected & that on the base of a masonry ~~pier~~ demolished pier. In the course of the night & the following day the lorry & gun traffic was very heavy.	

D. D. & L., London, E.C. (A8004) Wt. W1771/M2 31 750,000 5/17 Sch. 52 Forms/C2118/14

Instructions regarding War Diaries and Intelligence Summaries are contained in F. S. Regs., Part II. and the Staff Manual respectively. Title pages will be prepared in manuscript.

4

WAR DIARY
or
INTELLIGENCE SUMMARY.
(Erase heading not required.)

Army Form C. 2118.

Place	Date	Hour	Summary of Events and Information	Remarks and references to Appendices
			October 1918	
	19th		Completed odd details on LOCK GATE bridge, dismantled the pontoon bridge and moved to CHATEAU HAZEBROUCK near WERVICQ.	
	20th		Moved to billets in TOURCOING where the inhabitants gave the troops a most rousing reception which produced a most lasting impression on all ranks. The civilians had flags hanging out of nearly every house & deemed it an honour to be allowed to shake hands. In the billets the inhabitants could not do enough for the troops and then the Coy felt that they had had a certain degree of recompense for all the dreary & monotonous years spent on service. The reception & attitude of the inhabitants put new life into the men.	
	21st		Moved to billet 1 mile East of DOTTIGNIES.	

D. D. & L., London, E.C. (A8004) Wt. W1771/M2 31 750,000 5/17 Sch. 52 Forms/C2118/14

Army Form C. 2118.

Instructions regarding War Diaries and Intelligence Summaries are contained in F. S. Regs., Part II. and the Staff Manual respectively. Title pages will be prepared in manuscript.

5

WAR DIARY
or
INTELLIGENCE SUMMARY.
(Erase heading not required.)

Place	Date	Hour	Summary of Events and Information October 1918	Remarks and references to Appendices
	23rd		Moved to EVREGNIES taking over billets from 62nd Fd. Coy R.E.	
	24th		With help of 15 australians 2Lt SPENCER prepared the abutments & erected 1 trestle over the CANAL DE L'ESPIERRE and the adjoining river at 37/C 9c 2.5. Slightly [illegible] enemy in the vicinity.	
	25th		Took over work in line from 62nd Fd. Coy R.E.	
	25th to 29th		Built bridge at 37/C 9a 15.05 to take 7 tons axle load. as sketch.	
			Built 3 bridges for Inf. in single file at 37/C 9c 2.6. across canal & 2 streams.	
			Laid decking on bridge at 37/C 7c 8.4.	
			Put in intermediate trestles & decked bridge at 37/C 23 b 10.95. thus making it capable of taking vehicles of 12 tons axle load.	
			Prepared German floats for bridging purposes, & also 1 petrol tin bridge.	
	26th		No 4 Sect. under 2Lt SPENCER bridged stream at 37/C 7 b 6.5. in face of enemy opposition. Bridging completed & infantry occupied town on far side.	

D. D. & L., London, E.C. (A8004) Wt. W1771/M2731 750,000 5/17 Sch. 52 Forms/C2118/14

Instructions regarding War Diaries and Intelligence Summaries are contained in F. S. Regs., Part II. and the Staff Manual respectively. Title pages will be prepared in manuscript.

6

WAR DIARY
or
INTELLIGENCE SUMMARY.
(*Erase heading not required.*)

Army Form C. 2118.

Place	Date	Hour	Summary of Events and Information October 1918	Remarks and references to Appendices
	~~30th~~ 29th		With the 42nd Inf. Bde. a minor operation was planned to take place in 37/C10a & C4c with the view of establishing the line on the Eastern Bank of the ESCAUT CANAL.	
			Our forward posts were established at points marked X.	
			Floating bridge had previously been built at F & another at A.	
			Scheme proposed for a party of Inf. to cross at A & at a bridge to be built at B and then for the parties to work South & North respectively mopping up as they went.	
			After the operation was over it was proposed to build bridges at D & E in order to give access to island & to far bank.	
			At about zero + 20 mins. a party was ~~proposed~~ detailed to lay trench ladders across lockage piers at G & across the Lock.	
			Zero was fixed for 22 hours.	
			By 2-10 mins. a floating bridge consisting of [illegible] float piers & 10' trench boards, 80' total length, was put together at rt. angles to canal in a position indicated at C.	

A
ESCAUT
F
G
Lock
D
E
X
C
B
1500x

D. D. & L., London, E.C. (A8001) Wt. W1771/M2031 750,000 5/17 Sch. 52 Forms/C2118/14

Instructions regarding War Diaries and Intelligence Summaries are contained in F. S. Regs., Part II. and the Staff Manual respectively. Title pages will be prepared in manuscript.

7

WAR DIARY
or
INTELLIGENCE SUMMARY.

(Erase heading not required.)

Army Form C. 2118.

Place	Date	Hour	Summary of Events and Information — October 1918	Remarks and references to Appendices
	~~30~~ 21		From Z-10 to Z the bombardment of the Eastern Bank of canal continued by T.M.s - Stokes & 6" Newtons - At Z the Sappers assisted by 12 Australians picked up the bridge & launched it into the canal & had it ready for the infantry to pass at 10 minutes after zero - The scheme to bridge the [illegible] piers at G by means of crossed ladders was not a success as the span between the piers was greater than anticipated owing to the edges of the piers having been damaged - The party of Inf. assigned to cross here was diverted to bridge at B - At zero the party at A crossed successfully & rushed South - Summarising the operation was a complete success resulting in the capture of 7 unwounded prisoners, & the [illegible] of a number of Huns & our casualties being 4 wounded - At Z + 3½ hrs the bridging at D & 5 was commenced & completed at 05.30 hrs -	

D. D. & L., London, E.C.
(A8001) Wt. W1771/M2031 750,000 5/17 Sch. 52 Forms/C2118/14

Instructions regarding War Diaries and Intelligence Summaries are contained in F. S. Regs., Part II. and the Staff Manual respectively. Title pages will be prepared in manuscript.

8

WAR DIARY
or
INTELLIGENCE SUMMARY.
(Erase heading not required.)

Army Form C. 2118.

Place	Date	Hour	Summary of Events and Information — October 1918	Remarks and references to Appendices
		30th	Repaired bridges thrown across the ESCAUT last night –	
			Built bridge across the barrage gates & the Lock No 3 –	
			2 N.C.O.s & 2 Sprs patrolled tracks leading into the floods and found them impassable as there was 4' of water at about 1/2 way across swamps –	
		31st	Prepared further German floats & bridges – Took up floats, treadboards, & piles up to Lock No 3 in preparation for further operations –	
			2 Lieut R. H. TEATHER RE (T.C.) } reported for duty 4.10.18	
			2 Lieut A. W. HEAP RE. } 31.10.18 –	
			50 Australians of the 1st Aus. Siege Battery were attached to me from the 15th and proved of the utmost help in bridging operations –	
			1.11.18	
			E. C. W. Tempeley Major R E (TF) O. C. [illegible] Fd Coy R.E.	

D. D. & L., London, E.C. (A8001) Wt. W1771/M2031 750,000 5/17 Sch. 52 Forms/C2118/14

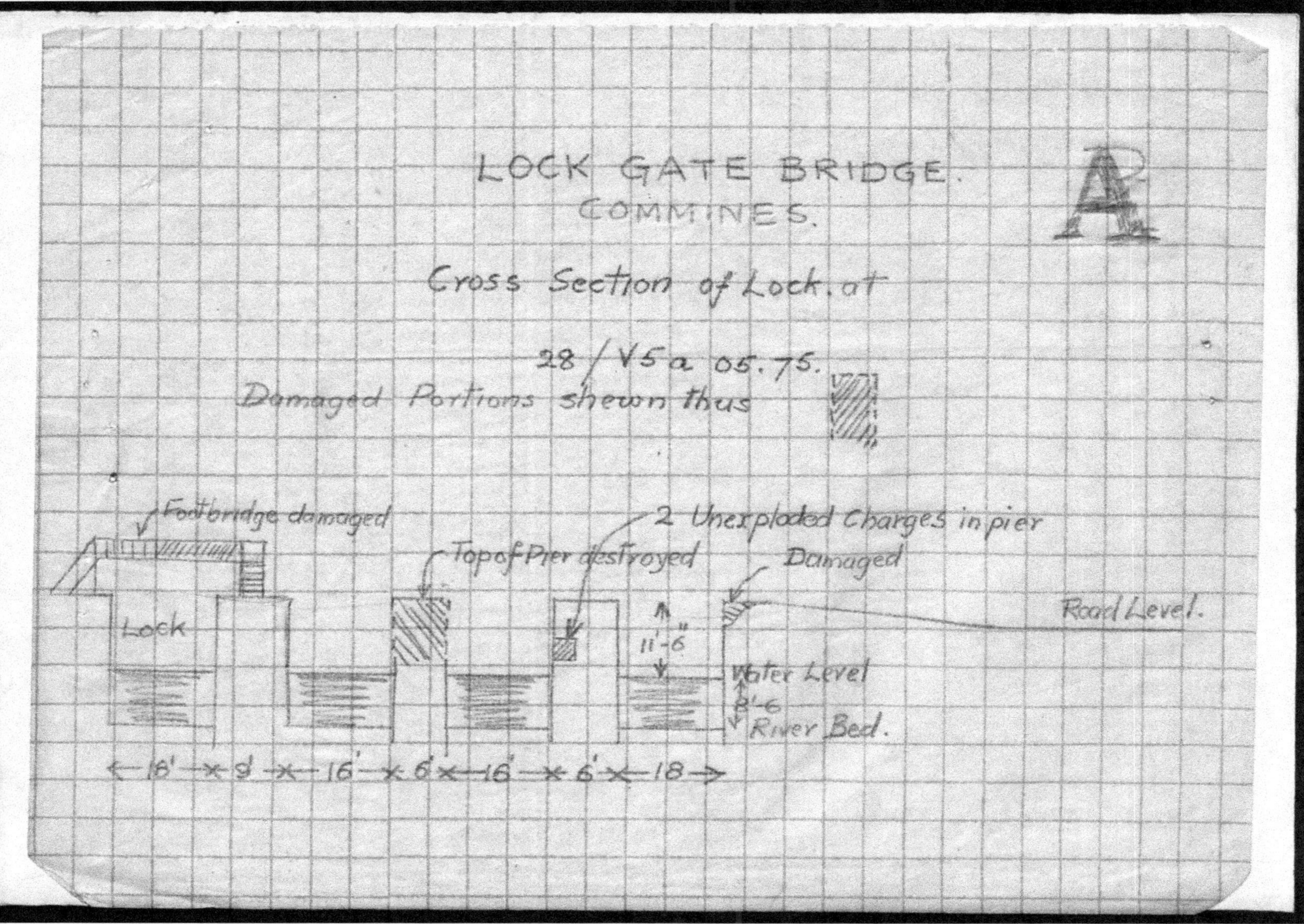

LOCK GATE BRIDGE.
COMMINES.
Cross Section of Lock at
28 / V5a 05.75.
Damaged Portions shewn thus
Footbridge damaged
Top of Pier destroyed
2 Unexploded Charges in pier
Damaged
Road Level.
Lock
11'-6"
Water Level
8'-6
River Bed.
18' 9 16' 6 16' 6' 18

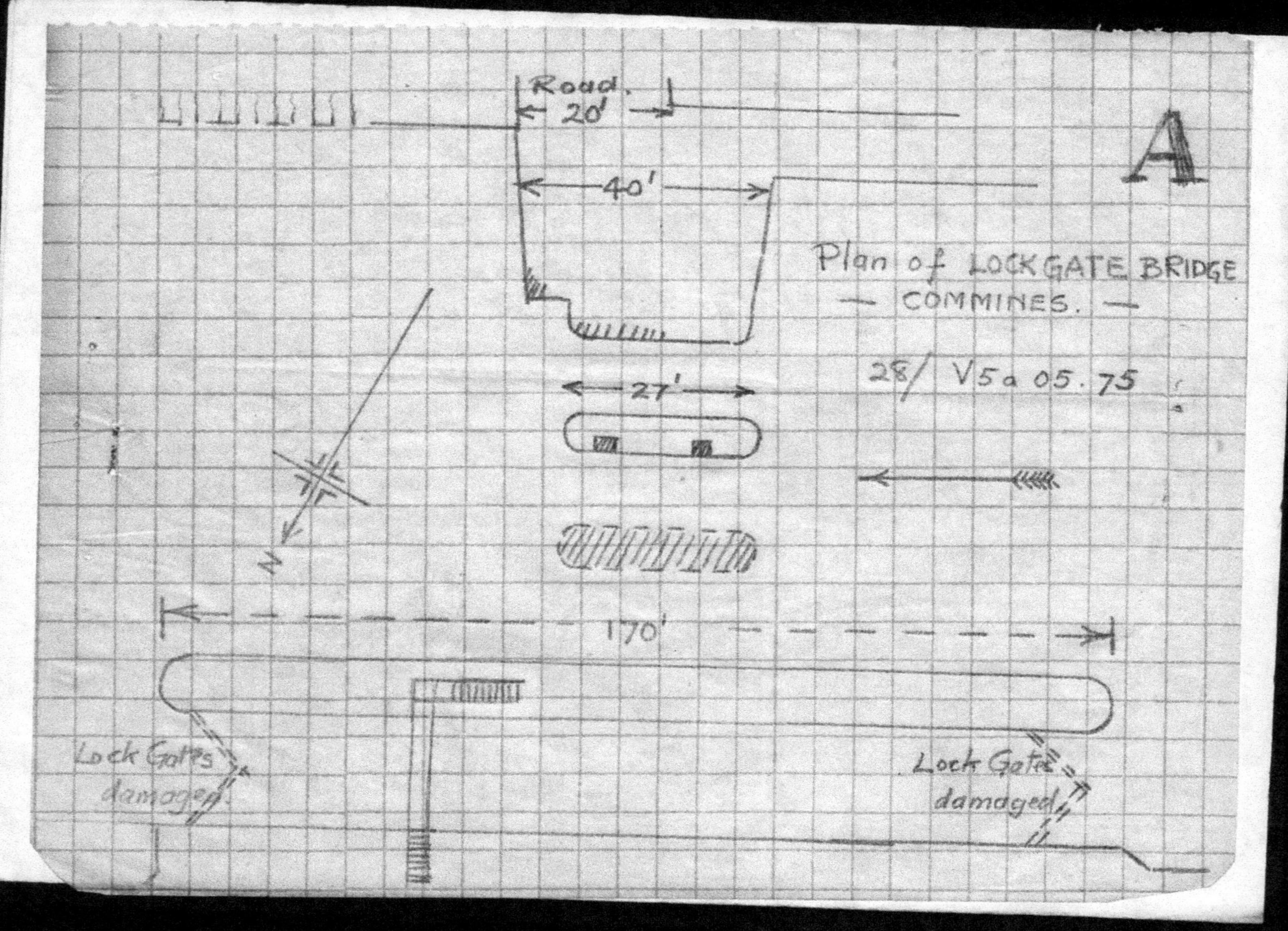
A
Plan of LOCKGATE BRIDGE
— COMMINES. —
28/ V5a 05.75
Road
20'
40'
27'
170'
N
Lock Gates damaged
Lock Gates damaged

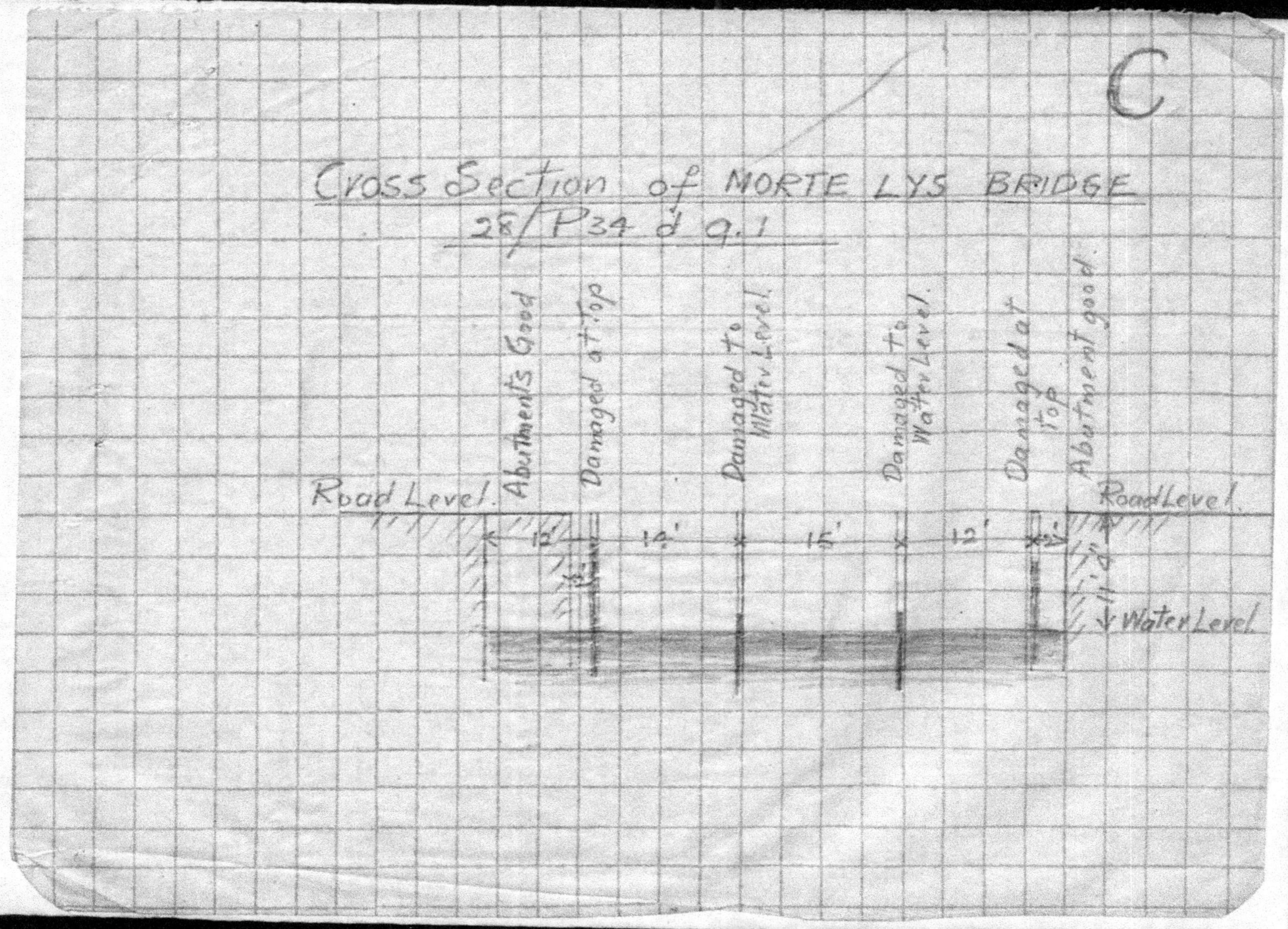
C
Cross Section of MORTE LYS BRIDGE
28/P34 d 9.1
Road Level.
Abutments Good
Damaged at top
Damaged to Water Level.
Damaged to Water Level.
Damaged at top
Abutment good.
Road Level.
12'
14'
15'
12'
11'-0"
Water Level

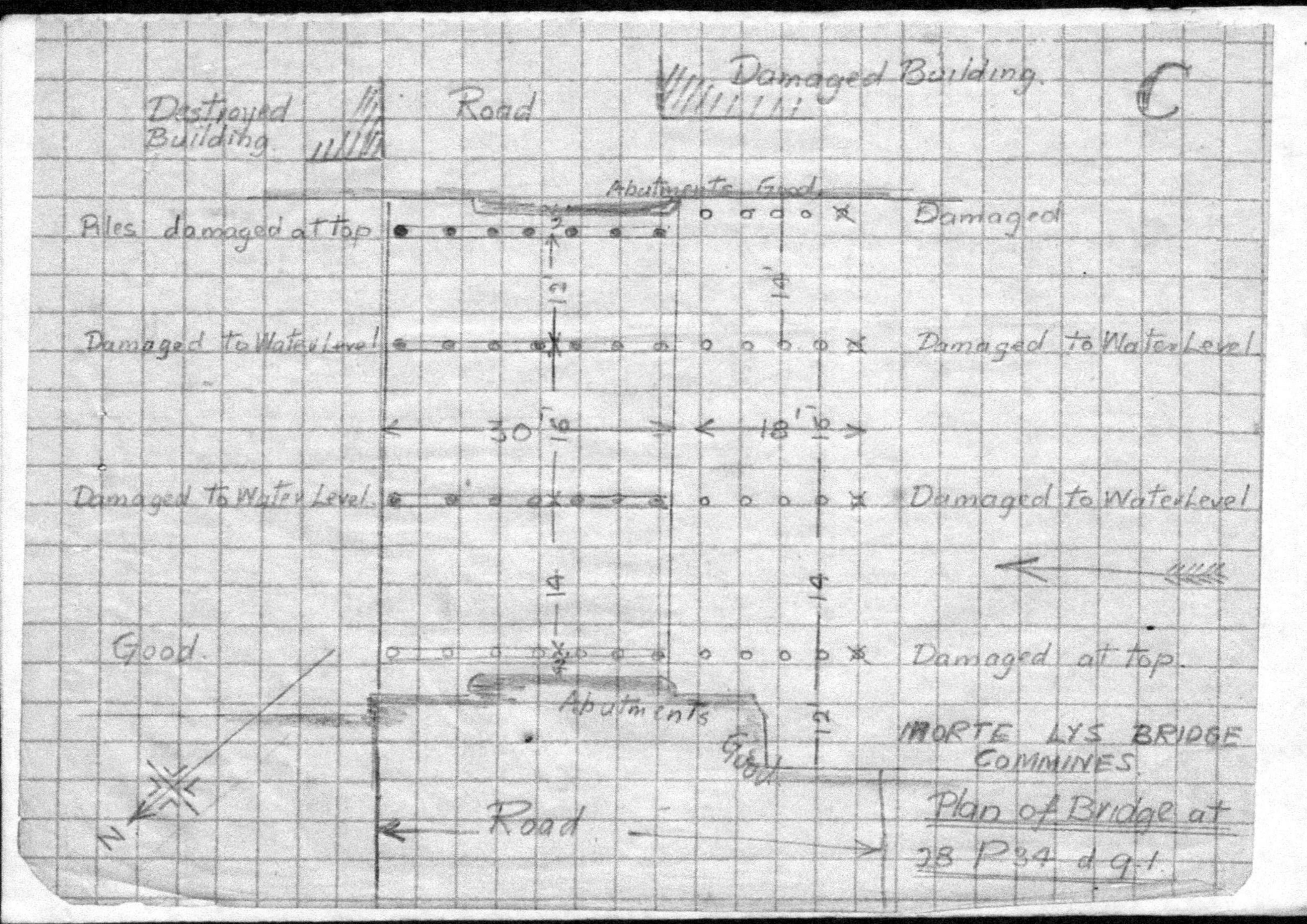
Destroyed Building
Road
Damaged Building
C
Abutments Good
Piles damaged at top
Damaged
Damaged to Water Level
Damaged to Water Level
30'
18'
Damaged to Water Level
Damaged to Water Level
14'
14'
Good.
Damaged at top.
Abutments
Good
MORTE LYS BRIDGE
COMMINES
Plan of Bridge at
28 P34 d 9.1.
Road
N

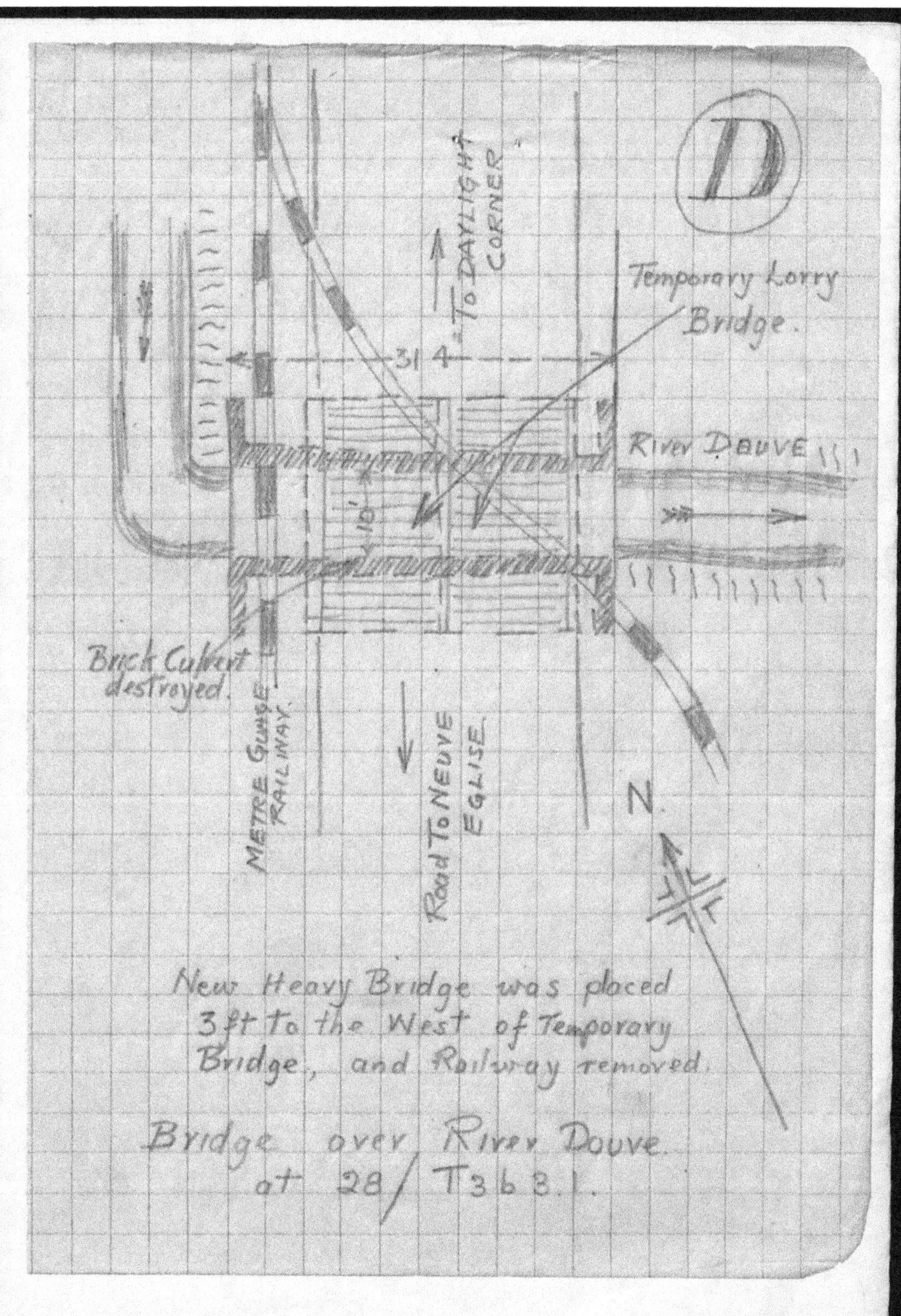
D
To DAYLIGHT CORNER
Temporary Lorry Bridge.
31 4"
River DOUVE
10'
Brick Culvert destroyed.
METRE GAUGE RAILWAY.
Road To NEUVE EGLISE
N.
New Heavy Bridge was placed 3ft to the West of Temporary Bridge, and Railway removed.
Bridge over River Douve. at 28/T3b3.1.

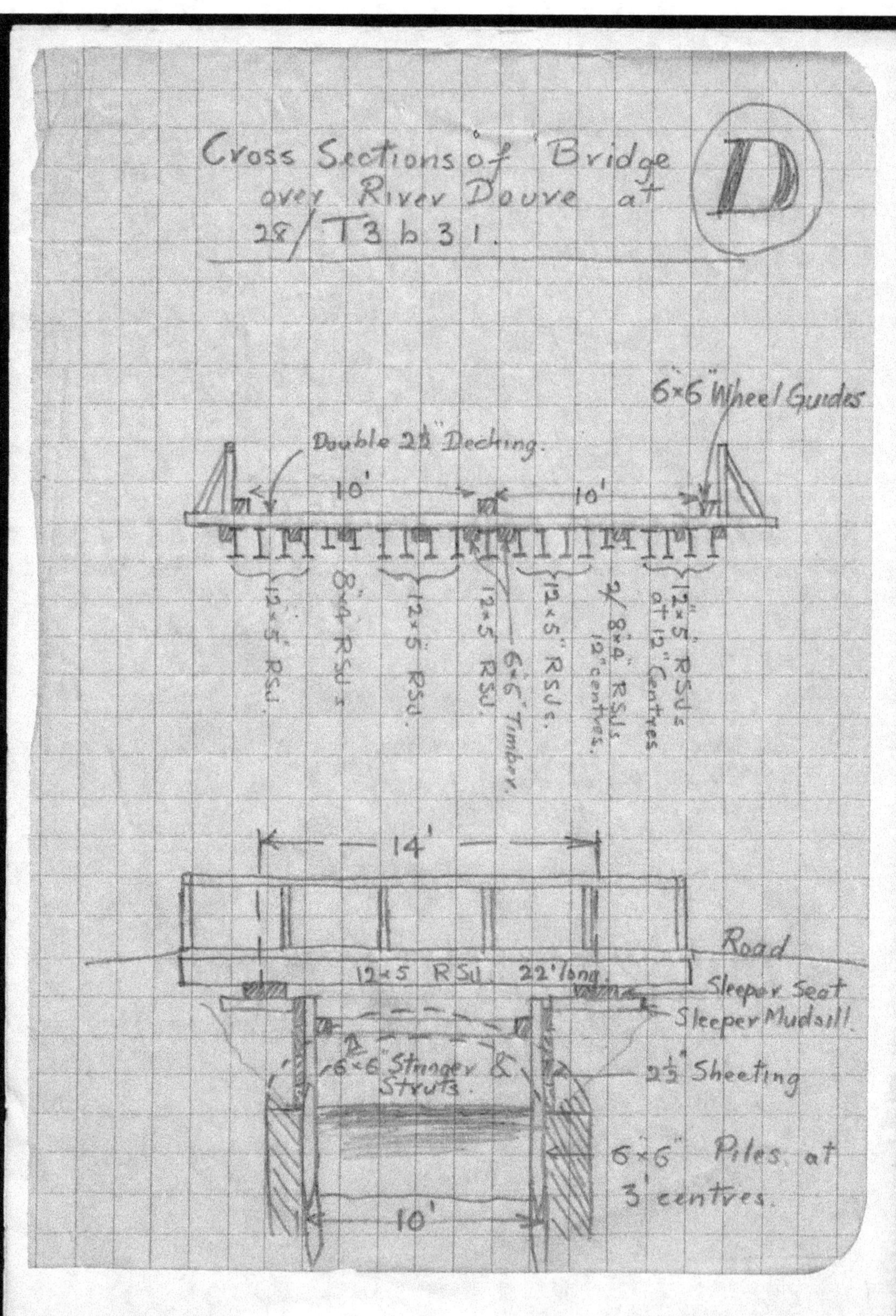

Cross Sections of Bridge over River Douve at 28/T3 b 31.
D
6×6" Wheel Guides
Double 2½" Decking.
10'
10'
12×5" RSJ.
8×4 RSJ s
12×5 RSJ.
12×5 RSJ.
6×6" Timber.
12×5" RSJs.
2/ 8×4" RSJs 12" centres.
12×5" RSJs at 12" Centres
14'
Road
12×5 RSJ 22' long
Sleeper Seat
Sleeper Mudsill.
2/ 6×6" Stringer & Struts.
2½" Sheeting
6×6" Piles at 3' centres.
10'

Army Form C. 2118.

61 Fd Coy R.E.

Instructions regarding War Diaries and Intelligence Summaries are contained in F. S. Regs., Part II. and the Staff Manual respectively. Title pages will be prepared in manuscript.

WAR DIARY
or
INTELLIGENCE SUMMARY.

(Erase heading not required.)

1

VIII 43

Place	Date	Hour	November – 1918 – Summary of Events and Information	Remarks and references to Appendices
EVREGNIES	1st		Prepared further German float bridge. Took up material to SUGAR FACTORY in preparation for bridging the ESCAUT – Repaired existing bridges.	
	2nd		As above with the addition that a bridge for pack animals was commenced over Lock No 3 at 37/C9 b 95.60.	
	3rd		Bridged the ESCAUT at SUGAR FACTORY at 37/C4 b 85.–80 [?]. Completed pack animal bridge at Lock No 3.	
	4th		Nos 2, 3, & 4 Sects assisted by the attached Australian Heavy Pontoons each built a German float bridge across the ESCAUT in the face of the enemy as below. This enabled Infantry to carry out very successful minor operation & capturing 19 Huns	& killing 15. Casualties to Brit. 4 –
			No 4 Sect. at 29/U30c 4.5 in 10 mins after zero. Width 95 feet.	
			No 2 Sect. at 29/U30c 80.95 in 1 hr 45 mins " " " "	
			No 3 Sect. at 29/U24 b 6.6 in 40 mins " " " "	
			Banks in first two cases formed approx. 12' to 14' in height & very nearly perpendicular – This enhanced the difficulty of launching – No 2 also bridged LANDBEEK at 29/U30a 4.9 –	
	5th		~~LAND~~ All bridges maintained and approaches improved –	

D. D. & L., London, E.C. (A8001) Wt. W1771/M2031 750,000 5/17 Sch. 52 Forms/C2118/14

Instructions regarding War Diaries and Intelligence Summaries are contained in F. S. Regs., Part II. and the Staff Manual respectively. Title pages will be prepared in manuscript.

2

WAR DIARY
or
INTELLIGENCE SUMMARY.
(Erase heading not required.)

Army Form C. 2118.

Place	Date	Hour	November 1918 – Summary of Events and Information	Remarks and references to Appendices
EVREENIES.	6th.		All 9 bridges in the front now existing in Div. front maintained & repaired –	
	7th.		Commenced making barrel pier bridge to be erected at 37/C9d 1.2.	
			Opened sluice into the ESCAUT at 29/U26b 5.3. in order to drain country round of the LANDBEEK. Canal is about 2 feet lower than LANDBEEK.	
			Attempted to construct new bridge across the ESCAUT at 29/U30c.1.5. but was unable to do so as the carrying party of Pioneers failed to turn up. This was not the Pioneers fault –	
			Other bridges repaired with the exception of No 1 bridge at 29/U30c 4.3 which was badly damaged by shell fire –	
	8th.		No 2 Sect. worked in day on barrel pier bridge with 10 Australians – All other Sects. were out at night with Australians – Barrel pier bridge across ESCAUT was nearly completed at 37/C9d 1.6. Bridge at 37/C4a 8.4 repaired – Bridge at SUGAR FACTORY removed & re-erected at 37/C5a 3.5 – New bridge thrown across ESCAUT at 29/U30c 2.6 with assistance of 89: Fd. C. R.E. (1 Sect.)	

D. D. & L., London, E.C. (A8001) Wt. W1771/M2031 750,000 5/17 Sch. 52 Forms/C2118/14

Instructions regarding War Diaries and Intelligence Summaries are contained in F. S. Regs., Part II. and the Staff Manual respectively. Title pages will be prepared in manuscript.

3.

WAR DIARY
or
INTELLIGENCE SUMMARY.
(Erase heading not required.)

Army Form C. 2118.

Place	Date	Hour	Summary of Events and Information — November 1918 –	Remarks and references to Appendices
EVREGNIES	8th		This bridge was launched with difficulty owing to M.G. fire up to 20.00 hours when enemy became quiet as they had left –	
	9th –	05.30am	Recd message from B.G.C. 4th Inf. Bde that they had retired, hence turned out 2Lt SPENCER & No 2 Sec to assist in crossing small streams on far side of ESCAUT – Informed 89th Fd. Coy R.E. –	
		07.50	Recd orders from C.R.E. to act in accordance with previously arranged orders regarding action to be taken in the event of enemy retiring – This consisted of assisting Infantry to cross stream in front of ESCAUT, & to construct mule track from Lock No 3, also HERINNES (?) to send 2 pontoons to 89th Fd Coy R.E. at HELCHIN – Mule track was completed at 18.00 hours – Pontoons dispatched at 10.00 hours & Infantry were assisted to cross – Coy moved to ESPIERRES.	
ESPIERRES	10th		Completed single way 8ft bridge across stream (10ft gap) at 37/L12 b 7.7. Assisted 62nd Fd Coy R.E. to complete heavy bridge at 37/C5 b 7.3. Salved lashings & tools from Infantry bridges.	

D. D. & L., London, E.C. (A8001) Wt. W1771/M2031 750,000 5/17 Sch. 52 Forms/C2118/14

Instructions regarding War Diaries and Intelligence Summaries are contained in F. S. Regs., Part II. and the Staff Manual respectively. Title pages will be prepared in manuscript.

WAR DIARY
or
INTELLIGENCE SUMMARY.
(*Erase heading not required.*)

Army Form C. 2118.

Place	Date	Hour	Summary of Events and Information	Remarks and references to Appendices
			November 1918.	
ESPIERRES.	11th		Completed double way 8ton bridge at 37/C12b77.	
			Commenced building causeway to INGLIS Bridge about to be erected at 37/C5&27. – Cut up felled trees for trestles & roadbearers. –	
			Hostilities ceased at 11.00 hours but this was not allowed to interfere with the work. –	
	12th		Continued work on causeway –	
	13th – 15th		Continued work on causeway, finishing on the 15th.	
	16th		Company less no 1 section moved to TOURCOING 90–92 Rue Admiral Courbet. Australian personnel of 2nd Australian Siege Battery rejoined their unit at TOURCOING.	
	17th		No 1 section repaired bridge at 37/B.18.c69 blocked main road beyond new causeway at 37/C5b37.	
TOURCOING.	18th		No 1 section rejoined company at TOURCOING.	
	20th		Company moved to Chateau d'Espierres 37/C2d82.	
ESPIERRES	21st–30th		Company employed on repairing village of ESPIERRES.	
			T. G. Hoking-Jones. Lt. R.E. for O.C. 61st Field Co. R.E.	

D. D. & L., London, E.C. (A8001) Wt. W1771/M2031 750,000 5/17 Sch. 52 Forms/C2118/14

Instructions regarding War Diaries and Intelligence Summaries are contained in F. S. Regs., Part II. and the Staff Manual respectively. Title pages will be prepared in manuscript.

WAR DIARY
or
INTELLIGENCE SUMMARY.

(*Erase heading not required.*)

Army Form C. 2118.

61 Fd Coy RE

'18

44

Place	Date	Hour	Summary of Events and Information	Remarks and references to Appendices
			DECEMBER	
"ESPIERES"	2.12.18 to 7.12.18		Company employed on repairing village of ESPIERES, Erecting ovens for (Company) cooking,	
	9.12.18 to 14.12.18		ditto " " " " " , Fitting up Ablution bench, Recreation, Lending Library and Reading-rooms. Erecting baths, and maintaining Bridges at 37/C.9.c.15.50, 37/C.7.c.85.35, 37/B18.a.50 + 37/B23.b.10.95.	
	16.12.18 to 21.12.18		Company employed on repairing village of ESPIERES. Fitting Dining-room for Company.	
	10.12.18		One II Cpl (MINER) returned to ENGLAND for demobilisation.	
	11.12.18		Two Drivers (MINERS) " " " " "	
	16.12.18		Two " ditto " " " "	
	23.12.18 to 31.12.18		Company employed on repairing village of ESPIERES. Repairing Bridge at 37/C.9.c.15.50. Repairs to Bridge at 37/B.18.a.5.0.	
	30.12.18		1 Sapper ("Pivotal") returned to ENGLAND for demobilisation	
	" "		1 Sapper ("Long Service") do " " " "	

31.12.18

E J Dowson Lieut RE
for O.C. 61st Field Co RE

D. D. & L., London, E.C.
(A8001) Wt. W1771/M2031 750,000 5/17 Sch. 52 Forms/C2118/14

61 Fd Coy R.E. 14

Army Form C. 2118.

Instructions regarding War Diaries and Intelligence Summaries are contained in F. S. Regs., Part II. and the Staff Manual respectively. Title pages will be prepared in manuscript.

WAR DIARY
or
INTELLIGENCE SUMMARY.

(Erase heading not required.)

61st Field Co R.E.

98 45

Place	Date	Hour	JANUARY 1919 Summary of Events and Information	Remarks and references to Appendices
ESPIERRES	1st to 31st		The company was employed in making minor repairs to houses in the village of ESPIERRES. The amount of work accomplished grew steadily less throughout the month owing to demobilization which was going on steadily at the beginning & in the middle of the month, & rapidly towards the end. At the 31st 101 men had been sent home for demobilization. In addition to which several were demobilised whilst on leave	

F. A. D. Richmond
Capt R.E.
for O.C. 61st Fd Coy R.E.

D. D. & L., London, E.C. (A8001) Wt. W1771/M2031 750,000 5/17 Sch. 52 Forms/C2118/14

Army Form C. 2118.

WAR DIARY
or
~~INTELLIGENCE SUMMARY.~~

Instructions regarding War Diaries and Intelligence Summaries are contained in F. S. Regs., Part II. and the Staff Manual respectively. Title pages will be prepared in manuscript.

FEBRUARY 1919 *(Erase heading not required.)*

Vol 46

Place	Date	Hour	Summary of Events and Information	Remarks and references to Appendices
ESPIERRES	1st		The company moved to billets in TOURCOING. During the month such men as were available for work, were employed on various small jobs, such as - a Prisoners of War Camp, wiring, making latrines etc; repairs to billets - some men were sent to assist 89th Fd Coy on construction of a bridge to take trams, across the Roubaix canal 1 officer & 15 O.R. were sent home for demobilisation during the month	

F. H. A. Reshmond
Capt R.E.
for O.C. 61st Fd Coy RE

D. D. & L., London, E.C.
(A8001) Wt. W1771/M2031 750,000 5/17 Sch. 52 Forms/C2118/14

CONFIDENTIAL.

WAR DIARY

- of -

61st FIELD COY., R. E.

1 - 31st March, 1919.

Instructions regarding War Diaries and Intelligence Summaries are contained in F. S. Regs., Part II. and the Staff Manual respectively. Title pages will be prepared in manuscript.

WAR DIARY
or
INTELLIGENCE SUMMARY.

(*Erase heading not required.*)

Army Form C. 2118.

Place	Date	Hour	MARCH 1919. Summary of Events and Information	Remarks and references to Appendices
TOURCOING.	1st-31st		Retainable men & Volunteers not already detailed out to join 231st Fd Coy R.E. 40 Div. This reduced the Coy to cadre strength except in officers. A few R.E. exhibits was carried out for Corps & Division.	

S. [illegible]
Major R.E.
O.C. 61 Fd Coy R.E.

61st FIELD COMPANY
Date 1.4.19.
ROYAL ENGINEERS

D. D. & L., London, E.C.
(A8001) Wt. W1771/M2031 750,000 5/17 Sch. 52 Forms/C2118/14

C O N F I D E N T I A L.

W A R D I A R Y

- of -

61st F I E L D C O Y., R. E.

From: 1st April, 1919.
To: 30th April, 1919.

61st Field Coy R.E.

Army Form C. 2118.

Instructions regarding War Diaries and Intelligence Summaries are contained in F. S. Regs., Part II. and the Staff Manual respectively. Title pages will be prepared in manuscript.

WAR DIARY
or
INTELLIGENCE SUMMARY.

(*Erase heading not required.*)

Place	Date	Hour	APRIL 1919 Summary of Events and Information	Remarks and references to Appendices
TOURCOING.	9th		4 men left unit for England	
"	12th		2 Lieut Goldfinch proceeded to 409th Field Coy. R.E. Army of occupation.	
	14th		Major E.E.V. Temperley MC RE(S.R) left for England for demobilization.	
	"		Capt F A B Richmond R.E from 62nd Field Coy to be O.C 61st Field Coy.	
	16th		Corps Commander XV Corps visited the Company. Several men complained to him of slowness of demobilization.	
	29th		Vacated TOURCOING & proceeded to billets at ESTAMPUIS.	
			No R.E work of any kind was carried out during this period.	
			R. H. Feather 2 Lieut RE. for O/C 61st Field Coy.	

D. D. & L., London, E.C. (A8001) Wt. W1771/M2031 750,000 5/17 Sch. 52 Forms/C2118/14

C O N F I D E N T I A L.

W A R D I A R Y

- of -

61st F I E D L C O M P A N Y, R. E.

From: 1st May, 1919.
To: 31st May, 1919.

Instructions regarding War Diaries and Intelligence Summaries are contained in F. S. Regs., Part II. and the Staff Manual respectively. Title pages will be prepared in manuscript.

WAR DIARY
or
INTELLIGENCE SUMMARY.
(Erase heading not required.)

Army Form C. 2118.

61st Field Coy. R.E.

Place	Date	Hour	Summary of Events and Information MAY 1919	Remarks and references to Appendices
STAMPUIS	1st to 31st		The cadre was waiting to go home. 10 men were demobilized during the month on reduction of cadre from 50 to 40 O.Rs.	F.A.A.R.
			F. A. A. Richmond Capt R.E. O.C. 61st Fd Coy R.E.	

D. D. & L., London, E.C. (A8001) Wt. W1771/M2031 750,000 5/17 Sch. 52 Forms/C2118/14

www.ingramcontent.com/pod-product-compliance
Lightning Source LLC
Chambersburg PA
CBHW060000240426
43662CB00038B/2087
* 9 7 8 1 4 7 4 5 0 8 7 3 5 *